KICK BOXING

A FRAMEWORK FOR SUCCESS

Pat O'Keeffe

CHIEF INSTRUCTOR MOD-KA KICK BOXING

CHIEF INSTRUCTOR MOD-KA KARATE-JUTSU

HEAD AND BRITISH TEAM COACH (K.I.C.K.)

About The Author

Pat O'Keeffe's first encounter with kick boxing was in the mid-seventies when as a private student he studied a blend of Goju Ryu karate and kick boxing under the legendary Steve Morris for some two years. Prior to this he had trained in karate, judo, ju-jitsu and aikido and currently holds a 4th dan in Mod-Ka karate-jutsu.

In April 1979 he met and started training under Geoff Britton, the then British B.A.F.C.A. team coach, and remained his student until 1989 when Geoff moved to Spain.

Whilst with Geoff Britton, Pat had twenty-eight kick boxing fights starting in October 1979 and finishing in October 1987. During this fighting career he fought three World Champions and the Belgian professional champion, Rudi Van Damme, a fight that appeared on *World of Sport*, the only time that kick boxing has been shown in a sports programme on terrestrial television.

Towards the end of his career he fought Nigel Benn the W.B.C. ex-World Professional Boxing Champion who was competing in both kick boxing and boxing at that time.

Since then Pat has officiated as both a judge and referee at every level in the sport including international events and has appeared on Meridian Television.

Now a successful trainer, he is presently the British head and team coach for the American kick boxing organisation K.I.C.K.

Acknowledgements

Special thanks to Ian Philips, 2nd dan Mod-Ka karate-jutsu, for the photography, to Ian Goodwin for his illustrations, and to my wife, Cathy, for the additional camera work - without their skills and patience this book would not have been possible.

Thanks also to my students Kabir Hussein, British W.A.K.O. Super lightweight Champion and W.K.A. Southern Area Super lightweight Champion, and Paul Mills for being the 'fall guys' in the photographs.

But most especially thanks to the man who appears throughout this book as my opponent, Frank Duffy, the assistant coach at Mod-Ka kick boxing and my right hand man, whose continued help and uncomplaining support across the years deserves more thanks than I could ever say.

This book is dedicated to my friend and teacher Geoff Britton,
who in the best Confucian tradition 'taught me to fish'.

First published 1997.
Revised edition published 1999
Reprinted 2000 and 2001

Summersdale Publishers Ltd
46 West Street
Chichester
West Sussex
PO19 1RP
United Kingdom

www.summersdale.com

Printed and bound in Great Britain.

ISBN 1 84024 093 8

Contents

Introduction

Kick boxing is an American child, born in the mid-seventies as a result of the creeping frustration felt by martial artists with the karate tournament circuit.

The seventies witnessed a martial arts revolution, partially brought about by western exposure to Chinese films and partially by the explosion of martial arts dojos, kwoons and dojangs throughout America and Europe. If the seventies had a creed it was 'Do your own thing!' and this social attitude spilt over into martial arts.

America has always been a melting pot of cultures and when the hunger for new martial arts experiences led to people sampling simultaneously, Japanese, Korean and Chinese martial arts, comparisons became inevitable.

Americans are iconoclasts by nature and did not hesitate to 'borrow' what was perceived as good in one style and add it to what they already had. Thus, Korean leg techniques became fused with Okinawan and Japanese hand techniques onto which the fluidity and subtlety of Chinese systems was grafted, in an attempt to create the 'ultimate style'. From these hybrids came many diverse systems, some good and some laughable.

This searching and experimentation caused considerable controversy, the ripples of which still can be detected, but then came what for many was a nightmare - full contact karate.

Full contact karate (not to be confused with Mas Oyama's dynamic Kyokushinkai fighting style) was a bastard derived from a dozen different styles with little or no etiquette and none of the discipline and mystique of traditional oriental fighting arts. Fighters entered a ring, wore boxing gloves and 'went for it'. These early pioneers could not have guessed what would follow. The simmering anger of traditionalists boiled over at this 'unruly child' who displayed none of the manners and ways of its parents. The very name 'Full Contact Karate' was attacked (and rightfully so given that what went on between the ropes was hardly karate) and yielding to the outcry, this new innovation increasingly used the term 'kick boxing'.

Yet the controversy was not all from the outside. When these 'kick boxers' entered the ring they discovered to their surprise if not horror, that their stamina was well below that needed to fight over several rounds. The reason for this was that the deadly techniques that they had practised all these years were largely negated when you placed boxing gloves on, and instead of 'one-punch kills' many blows were needed just to keep someone at bay.

Even the much-vaunted kicking techniques were nullified when your opponent closed in rapidly throwing haymakers at your head. Traditional blocking also proved to be suspect when blows came from all angles with real power behind the attacks.

The fights did not turn out to be deadly ballets, they were untidy, hard, exhausting brawls where good martial artists were reduced to wrecks by the sheer exertion of the contests.
Yet the clock could not be turned back.

Kick boxers turned to the yet another fighting system, western boxing. They watched with envy as professional boxers maintained their technique, their fitness and their cool over ten, twelve and even fifteen rounds. Clearly, if kick boxing was going to succeed it needed to go back to school and learn some secrets from boxers.

More than twenty years has elapsed since the first tentative steps of kick boxing's pioneers. It is now recognised as a martial sport in its own right, having links with the past, but making its own future.

Traditional arts have survived and in fact are now much stronger. Thus we now see karate styles, outwardly traditional, using hook and spinning hook kicks (Korean and Northern Chinese), spinning sweeps and takedowns, (Chinese) and openly examining other karate styles, adding and taking much in the process.

Kick boxing then is an eclectic martial sport that took twenty years in the making, shedding many skins to reach maturity. Like all sports, those who come after will be the best, each champion standing on the shoulders of the past champions, the pioneers who dared to try.

This book will aim to teach the techniques and skills to enable you to become a kick boxer or, if you are one already, to improve and deepen your skills. It will address all the areas that you will need if you are to reach your potential. It will require you to examine and analyse your own performance and that of your opponents, for only by ruthless self-searching and application can a fighter reach his or her potential.

My own teacher was Geoff Britton, a lateral thinker and clever martial artist to whom I owe a great debt, so I will open this book with a quote from him, a quote that like the man is both subtle and deep: 'The gym is your laboratory.'

Chapter One: The Fundamentals

STANCE AND GUARD

The target areas in kick boxing are the front and sides of the head and the trunk down to and including the line of the leggings. In order to prevent your opponent scoring on you an effective and appropriate guard is necessary. Further, in order to execute your own techniques you must maintain your balance. The correct combination of guard and stance will allow you to evade or attack fluidly.

1) **Full guard – Basic stance:** Stand with your feet one shoulder width apart, advance your left foot two feet, turn your body and feet slightly to your right and bend both knees. Raise your right heel. Place your gloves either side of your face so that they are just touching your cheek bones. Drop your chin slightly on to your chest. Your arms should be close to your body, elbows touching your ribcage. (Fig. 1)

2) **Cross guard – Basic stance:** Stand as in 1) but wrap your left arm across your stomach and your right across you upper chest. Drop your head forward so that a glove cannot fit either between your forehead and your arm or between your arms. Defend against an uppercut by leaning into it. (Fig. 2) This guard is best suited to a hooking specialist.

3) **Half guard – Basic stance:** Stand as in 1) but hold your upper left arm along the side of your body with your lower arm along the line of your leggings. Your right arm should be held tight into your side with the glove touching your cheekbone and your elbow touching your ribs. Your chin is protected by sandwiching it between your left shoulder and the right glove. (Fig. 3) This guard is very effective at close quarters and frees the left hand for both hooks and uppercuts.

4) **Half guard – Side straddle stance:** Your guard is the same as 3), but the feet are radically different. Stand sideways to your opponent with your feet three feet apart and your knees well bent. (Fig. 4) This is a stance specifically for a powerful sidekicker who wishes to make full use of that technique. Properly used, this stance can give the specialist kicker a real edge.

Fig. 1

Fig. 2

Fig. 3

Fig. 4

PRIMARY TOOLS: The most basic tools with which a fighter may enter a ring with any expectation of victory.

All techniques should be worked through slowly, only increasing in speed and power when the essentials have been mastered. Use a mirror to compare your form with the sequences shown and then progress to focus pads and the heavy bag. All punching and kicking techniques should accelerate throughout their execution and the force should be driven through the target.

Punching

There are four primary punches: 1) The jab
2) The cross
3) The hook
4) The uppercut

The Jab

The four essentials (Fig 5): 1) Chin down.
2) Right arm guarding.
3) Left shoulder touching the cheek.
4) Look along the arm like a gunsight.

Fig. 5

The jab is used in three ways:
1) As an intelligence gatherer.
2) As a point-scorer.
3) As a powerful stop-hit.

When used as an intelligence gatherer, the jab should probe your opponent's defences with a mixture of fast, hard and timed punches. These should be aimed at a variety of targets and thrown singly or in sharp bursts.

It is essential to note your opponent's reactions to these in order to ascertain whether he or she is a counter-puncher, aggressive, nervous, slow, skilful or clumsy. Having gathered this information you must use it to bring about your opponent's defeat.

As a point-scorer the jab is without parallel, being both fast and economical in terms of energy. It also opens the door for more powerful techniques.

When used as a stop/hit the jab should hit your opponent at the moment he begins his attack. The arm should be stiff at the end of the technique and jolt your opponent out of his stride.

The Head Jab

The sequence of the basic jab is shown in figs. 6 through to 8. The initiation should be explosive and the arm should return along the path it went out on to prevent being hit by a straight right hand counter.

Fig. 6

Fig. 7

Fig. 8

The Body Jab

A jab to the body is performed by bending the knees and moving your weight into the technique (Fig. 9). At no time should you merely aim downwards as this leaves you open to a strong right hand counter to the head.

A powerful body jab will force your opponent to drop his guard and thus create openings for other attacks. (See 'Chapter Four - Combinations')

The Angled Jab

The purpose of the angled jab is to defeat an orthodox and unchanging guard. By moving your body from left to right, up and down and circling your opponent, a jab may be fired in such a way that it is difficult or impossible for your opponent to catch or cover it. Below in figs. 10 through to 12 are various examples of this. A good fighter will always 'ask questions' of his opponent and without doubt a fast intelligent jab is the most efficient way of performing this.

Fig. 9   *Fig. 10*

Fig. 11   *Fig. 12*

The **rising jab** (Fig. 13) and the **dropping jab** (Fig. 14) are extensions of the angled jab and should be used in the same way.

Mastery of the jab is the hallmark of a champion. Used correctly, there is no more versatile weapon in a kick boxer's arsenal.

Fig. 13

Fig. 14

Fig. 15

Fig. 16

Fig. 17

The Cross

'The spoon that digs the meat out...'

The cross is a straight punch delivered with the rear hand to both the head and the body. The difference between a jab and a cross was summarised by my army sergeant thus: '. . . the jab is the can opener and the cross is the spoon that digs the meat out!'

The sequence of the basic cross is shown in figs. 15 to 17.

The left arm is kept in tight to the side and the body rotates to enable the right hand to reach its target. The rear foot moves half a pace forward to place body weight behind the punch.

If the limb of a fighter can be considered the missile, then the body is the 'warhead'. The more weight behind the technique then the greater the damage inflicted. The half-step performed by the rear foot should be as fast as possible.

The cross should never be thrown 'cold'. Use it as part of a combination or as a 'timed' counter-punch.

The Body Cross

Like the jab, the cross to the body should be accompanied by a bending of the knees (Fig. 18). The targets for a body cross are primarily the liver and the solar plexus. (See the Appendix – Targets and Techniques)

Fig. 18

The Overhand Cross

This is the tool of the experienced fighter and can be a devastating blow. It is thrown in the same way as the basic cross except that it loops over the top rather than in a straight line. It is best employed against an opponent's jab when you catch him coming in, thereby doubling the impact of the blow. (Fig. 19)

Strictly speaking an overhand cross falls into the category of a 'meet' - that is a blow thrown at the same time as your opponent's, without first parrying or blocking and using a slipping body motion to evade the blow aimed at you.

Fig. 19

The Short Cross

The short cross is a subtle close-range blow that is thrown without the half-step of the rear foot. The rear arm is merely straightened in a sawing motion (Figs. 20 to 22). Its power is derived from timing and it is particularly effective as no set up is needed that might 'telegraph' your intent to your opponent.

Fig. 20   *Fig. 21*   *Fig. 22*

The Hook

Fig. 23

The hook is a curved blow whose purpose is to defeat your opponent's guard by going around it. Hooks can be used at long, medium or short-range, although it is primarily a short-range technique.

Hooks can be thrown with either the lead or the rear hand and, because of their circular path of attack, are very strong. When used together with straight punches they 'test' an opponent's guard to the maximum.

Fig. 24

The sequence of the lead hook to the head is shown in figs. 23 to 25. The lead ankle, hip and shoulder turn explosively into your opponent. The elbow is kept high and the hand rotates so that the thumb is towards you. Your hand leaves the guard at the last possible moment so that your opponent has no time to 'read' it.

The final position is with your chin tucked down, your elbow high so that you are peering over it, and your body sideways to your opponent.

Fig. 25

The Body Hook

The body hook is an excellent way of weakening your opponent. The technique is performed the same way as the basic hook except that the blow is delivered by rapidly bending both knees at the moment of throwing. (Fig. 26)

Fig. 26

The Shovel Hook

This technique falls halfway between a hook and an uppercut. It is thrown the same as a hook except that the angle of attack is 45 degrees (Fig. 27). It is a superb weapon when aimed at the liver (Fig. 28) or the solar plexus (Fig. 29). I recommend its use as a 'meet' against a jab or as part of a combination.

Fig. 27

Every serious kick boxer should practise the shovel hook until it is second nature. It is one of the big ones.

Fig. 28

Fig. 29

The Rear Hook

Essentially this is thrown in the same way as the basic hook, although obviously the body has to rotate more. Ensure your elbow finishes high, otherwise your chin will be on offer. (Fig. 30)

It is a heavy blow and can inflict great damage. However, because of the extra rotation needed to deliver it, and the subsequent opening up of your trunk target areas to your opponent, it should never be used 'cold'. Use it as part of a combination or, if you are very skilled, as a 'timed' counter-attack.

Fig. 30

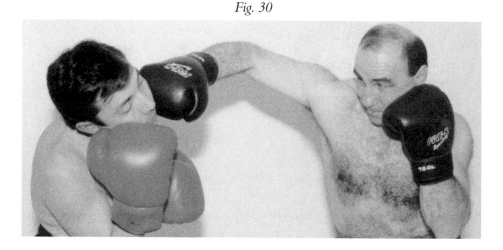

The Long-Range Hook

This technique calls for a committed delivery with a looping attacking arm. It is not a wild swing, but a precise tool that can be used to entice your opponent into a wide block and therefore leaves him open to follow-up blows. (Figs. 31 and 32)

Fig. 31   *Fig. 32*

The greater distance travelled by the punch makes it very strong. It is best thrown as your opponent retreats so that his weight is going backwards and he does not have the opportunity to slip inside your guard and counter you.

Fig. 33

The Spring Hook

The spring hook is thrown after you have ducked an attack, leaving both your knees bent and therefore potentially full of explosive power. After ducking, throw the hook as normal, but rise rapidly upward as you do so, striking your opponent's chin with maximum force. Practise this on the heavy bag, making the bag 'jump' when you hit it. (Figs. 33 and 34)

Fig. 34

The Uppercut

The uppercut is best thought of as a vertical hook, in that the ankle, hip and shoulder rotate in exactly the same manner, except that the hand rises upward between your opponent's arms to attack either the head or the body. (Figs. 35 to 37)

Fig. 35

Fig. 36

It cannot be emphasised enough that this rotation should be explosive. It is best employed when your opponent leans forward or has just ducked an attack. An especially effective method of use is when throwing the rear uppercut from outside your opponent's jab. (Fig. 38) His own arm will blind him to the attack until the last minute when it comes from underneath and strikes his chin.

Fig. 37

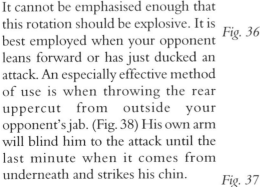

Fig. 38

You should experiment with hooks, shovel hooks and uppercuts so that you can attack your opponent through 360 degrees. A variety of punches will keep him guessing, thereby robbing him of the initiative and placing him in the position of always having to 'solve' you, rather than the other way round.

It is impossible to list and illustrate all the variables of attack with the basic punches, however mastery of all the punches above is rare, even in champions. Set yourself the goal of working through the basics, from bag, to pads to sparring to actual fights in the ring. Add the variations gradually, experimenting on less skilled fighters until you can do those techniques you feel will serve you best.

It should be remembered that a martial artist always strives to increase his technical range, whereas a fighter's main aim is effectiveness, which may mean a relatively small range of techniques, but each one fast and powerful with subtle variations to stretch the opponent.

Kicking

Potentially, kicks are the most powerful weapons available to a fighter.

The leg is longer and stronger than the arm. With practice it also becomes faster. Unless you are an exceptional kicker, (and if you have to stop to think about this then you are not) your legs should always follow your hands in a combination. Leading with a kick is too large a motion to start an attack and you must expect to get heavily countered if you use a kick 'cold'.

Weak kicks serve no purpose, halve your stability and momentarily prevent you from moving. Further, the energy expenditure of a kick is too great for you to squander it. If it's worth kicking it's worth kicking hard.

Timing a kick is a subtle skill and many never acquire it. Train all kicks on the big bag in order to develop raw power, later progress to the focus pads for speed and variety.

There are five primary kicks:
1) Lead front kick
2) Lead roundhouse kick
3) Rear roundhouse kick
4) Back thrust kick
5) Lead side kick

All the primary kicks should be thrown to the body, which is a larger and less mobile target area than the head. An examination of kick boxing leg techniques will reveal that 80 per cent of effective kicks are to the body using the above-named kicks.

This is not to say that other techniques are not effective, merely that you should aim to first acquire those which stand the greatest chance of success.

It cannot be stated enough that a high, flamboyant eye-pleasing kick that fails to hurt your opponent is the tool of the egotist. A hard, punishing body kick on the other hand will weaken your opponent, bring down his guard (leaving his chin open) and of course, score points.

You must be disciplined. Reject anything that does not gain you an advantage. If you want to win you must be ruthless . . . with yourself.

Lead Leg Front Kick

This kick is arguably the simplest, fastest and the most economical in terms of energy expenditure. It can be thrown at long and medium-range, but is especially effective when thrown at close-range to the pit of the stomach.

The sequence for a lead leg front kick is as follows: without altering your guard quickly place you rear foot just behind your front heel; lift your front leg and point the knee at the middle of the body on the line of his leggings; snap the foot forward, driving your hips behind it; make contact with the ball of the foot. (Figs. 39 to 41)

Fig. 39

Fig. 40

Fig. 41

When used defensively merely pick up the front leg and drive it in hard.

Practise this kick on the big bag by swinging the bag away from you and at the precise moment of its starting to return, drive your kick explosively forward. Aim to make the bag jump rather than swing away.

Fig. 42

To practise the close-in version, stand so that your guard is touching the bag (Fig. 42). Push yourself back slightly and draw your knee up close to your chest (Fig 43). Stab the kick home.

As stated above, the target for this kick is on the line of the leggings and in the middle of the body. This is because there is a natural outward slope of the forearms in the guard position and a large target area is presented. (Fig. 44)

Fig. 43

Occasionally an opportunity to throw this kick to the head presents itself, for example when your opponent dips forward due to fatigue or a body shot. In these circumstances the kick is devastating and can end a fight.

Fig. 44

Fig. 45

Fig. 46

Fig. 47

Lead Leg Roundhouse Kick

The lead and rear leg roundhouse kicks should be thought of as hooks performed with the leg. Their aim is the same, to come around your opponent's guard.

The lead roundhouse kick is performed by raising your lead leg as in the lead front kick. Next, pivot on your rear leg and throw the foot in an arc towards your opponent's side. Contact is made with the instep or if you prefer, the shin. (Figs. 45 to 47)

The target is the gap between your opponent's right elbow and the line of his leggings. This gap occurs even in the tightest of defences because frequently fighters fail to take account of its existence. Assume a normal full guard in the mirror and observe it for yourself.

Power is obtained by rapidly turning the support leg, snapping the front knee and strongly rotating your hip. Further power can be gained by lunging in behind the kick.

Rear Leg Roundhouse Kick

This kick is the Exocet Missile of kick boxing. Tremendous power can be generated with this technique and considerable time should be spent developing it on the big bag.

The sequence for the rear roundhouse kick is as follows: pick up your rear leg horizontally, with the knee tucked in. Pivot sharply on the support leg and drive your hip forward. At the same time, snap your knee straight and your rear foot will propel itself in an arc towards the target. (Figs. 48 to 50)

As with the lead roundhouse kick the target area is the gap between the elbow and the line of the leggings.

There are many variations on the basic roundhouse kick, each one devised for a set purpose. Practise them on the big bag and gradually introduce them into your sparring.

Fig. 48

Fig. 49

Fig. 50

Sidestep Roundhouse Kick

This is performed by taking a pace at a 45 degree angle towards your opponent and firing the kick in across the front of his body. (Figs. 51 and 52)

Fig. 51   *Fig. 52*

The angle makes the kick very strong and when used as part of a combination it can finish off your opponent.

Body Shift Roundhouse

This is performed for the same reason as the sidestep roundhouse with added power coming from the 'jump' and subsequent total commitment of body weight behind the kick.

The sequence for this kick is as follows: perform a low jump/skip towards your opponent at 45 degrees, throwing your kick across his body as you do so. (Fig. 53)

The 'body shift' places all your weight behind the technique and maximises your power. Thai Boxers use this kick to great effect. They use the full length of a toughened shin to strike with, and it has to be felt to be appreciated.

Fig. 53

The Disguised Roundhouse

This is performed by raising the rear leg as though performing an orthodox rear Front kick, but on throwing it you suddenly pivot on your support leg and send your foot forward in an arc.
(Figs. 54 and 55)

Fig. 54

Fig. 55

The power of this kick is not as great as the basic roundhouse or the sidestep and body shift variants, however it makes up for it by being faster and much harder to 'read'.

The Spinning Backthrust Kick

This kick is potentially the strongest of all kicks. Its power is derived by use of rotational power followed by a violent thrusting of the leg in a straight line by some of the biggest muscles in the body.

Because you momentarily turn your back on your opponent, it is essential that you emphasise the head turn prior to the kick. Further, if it is generally true that your hands should set your legs up, then it is doubly so with this technique.

The sequence for the spinning backthrust kick is as follows:

Spin 180 degrees on the ball of your front foot, ensuring you turn your head, shoulders and hips ahead of your leg.

Pick your rear leg up to the side, aiming your heel at your opponent.

Extend the leg in a straight line towards your opponent's midsection.

Make contact with the heel of the foot. (Figs. 56 to 58)

Fig. 56

Fig. 57

Fig. 58

Fig. 59

There are several variations on this kick, including simply throwing the foot without picking the leg up first, in order to disguise the kick. (Fig. 59)

Power training on the big bag for this technique is essential, however, I suggest that an equal amount of time is spent on the focus pads to ensure accuracy. It is the best of all the finishing blows and time spent in acquiring it will not be wasted.

Fig. 60

Fig. 61

Fig. 62

Fig. 63

The Lead Leg Side Kick

The virtues of the lead leg side kick are many. It is the perfect stop-hit, (that is a technique that you throw the very moment your opponent launches an attack and either stops him or throws out his timing) and it is also a very economical way of hitting your opponent without becoming involved. Further, it is second only in speed to the front kick and second only in power to the spinning back thrust.

Not enough people spend time developing this technique – it is interesting to note that the Americans are an exception. When coupled with a half guard - side straddle stance (see page 8) this technique can dictate the terms of a fight.

The sequence for throwing it is as follows: bring you rear foot up and place it behind the heel of your front foot. Pick up you lead leg and turn the leg sideways to your stance. Extend your leg towards your opponent's midsection and make contact with your heel (Figs. 60 to 62). On completion of the kick your ankle, knee, hip and shoulder should all be in a straight line. (Fig. 63)

This kick can be used defensively (as a stop-hit) by eliminating the step and merely picking up your front leg and powering the kick home.

Again the tool to sharpen this technique is the big bag, but focus pad work will add snap and accuracy.

The Foot Sweep

The foot sweep is a throw effected by using the sole of your foot to knock your opponent's foot out from under him.

This does not count as a knockdown under most rules, however, it does upset your opponent and robs him of the confidence to commit fully behind his techniques.

When combined with kicks and punches it is an excellent way of weakening your opponent's defence. Also, there is a tendency for your opponent to throw out his hands for balance when swept, thus allowing the fast fighter to score heavily on the unprotected target areas.

Timing is of the essence when throwing a sweep. The best times are just as your opponent moves forward, as he places his foot down after kicking, when he attempts a head kick and his support leg is presented, and as mentioned before, as part of an overall combination.

The sequence is as follows: keeping your guard high and your gaze around his chest area, throw your foot in a sweeping arc, connecting with the sole of your foot against the foot of your opponent. (Fig. 64)

Drive through with plenty of hip action.

A sweep may be performed to the inside of your opponent's foot although this is not allowed under some rule systems. Also most rules systems require a sweep to be used at no more than boot height.

Sweep practice can be performed on a light bag hung just off the floor. Increase the size (weight) of the bag until you can displace a big bag.

Fig. 64

It cannot be overemphasised that attainment of the basic skills should be your first aim, adding the variations only when you have done so. That said, the fighter must never be a clone and experimentation will give you your individuality.

Once you have acquired an understanding of the principles and mechanics of each technique, then you must work them until they are second nature. It should be engraved on each kick boxer's heart that it takes 5,000 repetitions to make a physical action an instantaneous reflex.

Your skills must surface when you are tired, hurt and confused. When that tiny voice inside your head is telling you to lie down. Quite simply, your skills must not be smothered under pressure, but released by it.

Chapter Two: Secondary Tools

In this chapter we will examine a further selection of techniques that will broaden your skills and thereby create more options in attack. We will also include head kicks for the first time.

I don't intend to suggest at any time that head kicks are inferior to body kicks, merely that you stand a greater chance of connecting with body kicks. That said, we must now state that when they connect, head kicks frequently result in the finish of the fight.

Also we will examine two additional hand techniques. The first of these, the bolo punch comes from boxing, yet it rarely appears in boxing texts and is frequently not identified as a separate technique.

The other hand technique shown in this section is the spinning backfist and is derived from eastern martial arts. Although used in karate and semi-contact competition, it is in kick boxing that this technique has found its natural home.

The Bolo Punch

Many people confuse the bolo punch with an uppercut, mainly because it targets the same areas and is used in similar situations. However, there the similarity ends.

The uppercut draws its power from an explosive twist of the ankle, hip and shoulder. The glove does not leave your guard until the last possible moment. (See page 19, Figs. 35 to 37)

The bolo on the other hand is a large looping punch that gains its power from a whipping motion caused when you shorten the arc of the loop.

It is a good tool for the long-limbed fighter who has to adapt to find a solution when a smaller opponent continually attempts to take the fight to close-range.

Because its action is large, the timing of a bolo is crucial. Throw it as your opponent steps forward.

The sequence for the bolo is as follows: as your opponent presses in, take a half pace back with your rear foot and throw your rear hand in a loop until it reaches your hip. Now, shorten the arc and whip the punch in under the ribcage. (Figs. 65 to 67)

As stated before, to the untrained eye the bolo looks like a loose uppercut. Try both on the focus pads and in sparring and you will learn the difference.

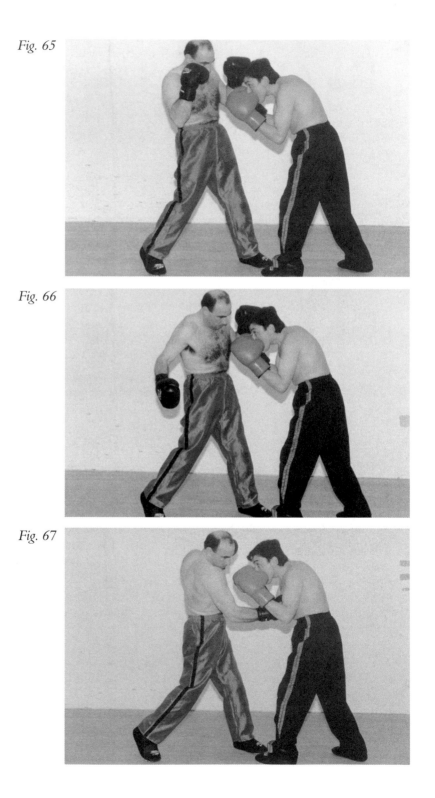

Fig. 65

Fig. 66

Fig. 67

The Spinning Backfist

This technique has the triple attributes of speed, power and deception. It should be used sparingly as an ambush. All too often fighters squander the uniqueness of this technique by continually throwing it for the wrong reasons.

Although there are many ways it can be used, for the novice fighter I strongly recommend that you throw the spinning backfist after an effective jab or when close-in and your opponent has little time to see it.

Fig. 68

The sequence is as follows: spin 180 degrees on your front foot, keeping your arm raised and tight into your chest. Remember to turn your head, shoulders and hips ahead of the technique. Release your arm and let your body propel it round in a fast arc. Make contact with the knuckle part of the glove on the jaw or temple. (Figs. 68 to 70)

Fig. 69

Failure to turn your head will result in your not focusing on the target and possibly hitting your opponent with your forearm or elbow. Either could get you disqualified.

Fig. 70

The spin should be smooth and fast. The focus pad is the right equipment for learning this technique. Throw the jab and then turn into the spinning backfist. Start slowly, ensuring that there is no jerkiness or stiffness in the action.

The Rear Front Kick

Fig. 71

It is possible to liken the lead front kick to a jab with the leg, and therefore the rear front kick to a straight right cross.

It is true to say that when you rotate your body in throwing a right cross, you are turning your target areas towards your opponent and the same must be said of the rear front kick. It is essential therefore when throwing this kick (or any other kick for that matter) to keep your arms tight together.

Fig. 72

The sequence is as follows: pick up your rear leg and aim your knee at your opponent's midsection. Snap the kick forward and drive your hips behind it. Finish with your arms tight in front of you and your leg fully extended. (Figs. 71 to 73)

Fig. 73

The line of attack is straight in, not rising, and the contact area is the ball of the foot.

All straight kicks seriously weaken your opponent when they are driven home. It is important to remember that when your opponent moves forward, only straight-in kicks that hit into his line of attack should be used.

A round or circular technique used against a forward moving opponent is at best a gamble and at worse an open invitation to be countered heavily.

The Roundhouse Kick to the Head

This technique is one that is seen often in the ring and arguably is the most commonly used 'head shot'.

Frequently this kick will fail because the correct action is not used, resulting in the line of attack going through your opponent's shoulder and therefore failing to hit the target.

The knee must be raised high and the line of attack made to defeat the instinctive defence of the 'shoulder raise'. (See 'Chapter Three - Defensive Skills')

The sequence is as follows: pick up your rear leg with the knee high and pointing at your opponent's head. Pivot sharply on the support leg and drive your hip forward. At the same time snap your knee straight and throw your foot in an arc towards the target. Make contact with the instep or shin.
(Figs. 74 and 75)

Fig. 74

The same variations for the body roundhouse can be used for the head version. There is however one additional variation which is derived from Thai Boxing.

Fig. 75

The Crocodile Kick

This technique can be described as a descending roundhouse(!)

It is possible for your opponent to rob your roundhouse of power by swaying his upper body away from the kick so that although you may make contact, it is only a glancing blow.

To defeat this, pick your leg up high and send your kick over in a descending loop. Strike your opponent in the neck as he sways downward. (Fig. 76)

Fig. 76

Practise this with a partner, controlling the power until you have learnt to adjust the path correctly. Then substitute a focus pad and build up to full power delivery. (Fig. 77)

Fig 77

The Hook Kick

This kick has an unusual path of delivery and is hard for your opponent to see unless he spots it early. The front leg version is the most commonly used, although I have found that the back leg version is more deceptive and therefore harder still for your opponent to read.

This kick is an excellent weapon with which to ambush your opponent. Use it sparingly to enhance the surprise factor. The focus pad is the tool for sharpening the hook kick.

The Front Leg Hook Kick

This technique is designed to defeat your opponent's guard by coming around it. The degree of hook that you put in the technique can be varied, making it very difficult to successfully defend against.

The sequence is as follows: place your rear foot behind your front foot. Pick up your front leg and bend it so that it is close into your chest. Throw the kick out in an arc, hooking the knee to come around your opponent's guard. Make contact with the heel. (Figs. 78 to 80)

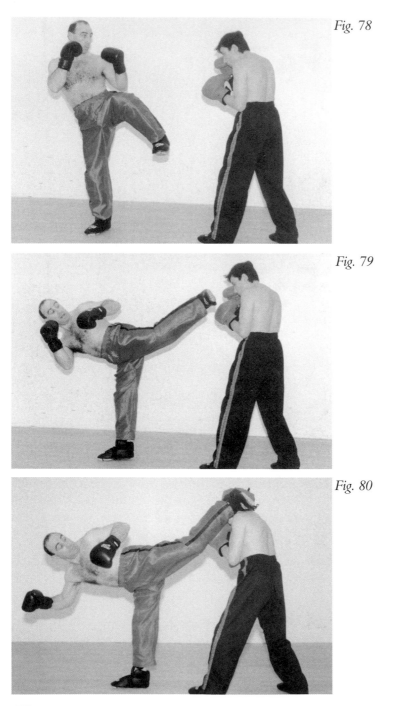

Fig. 78

Fig. 79

Fig. 80

There are two main variations of the lead leg hook kick.

The Side Hook Kick

This variation uses a lead side kick action. Throw the kick exactly as you would a high lead leg side kick, but slightly off to one side of your opponent's head. As the kick comes in line with the guard, bend your knee and strike home with the heel. (Figs. 81 and 82)

Fig. 81   *Fig. 82*

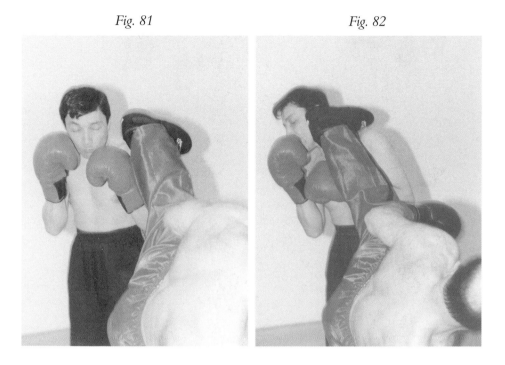

The main advantages of this variation are that the kick is faster and the path of delivery is very deceptive, luring your opponent into thinking that it is a side kick that has missed.

The Straight Leg Hook Kick

Arguably, this is not a hook kick at all, however I have included it here because superficially it resembles a hook kick and can be used in similar circumstances.

Also unless you intend to use the hook kick it is unlikely that you will add this to your range of techniques.

The main feature of this variation is that the kicking leg remains straight throughout. Because of the lack of hooking action it is easier for your opponent to see, therefore it is used as a finishing blow rather than to open an attack.

The sequence is as follows: step up behind your lead foot. Keeping the leg straight, raise and throw your heel in an arc towards your opponent's head. Drive the kick through the target with a powerful hip action. (Figs. 83 and 84)

Fig. 83

Fig. 84

The Rear Leg Hook Kick

Raise your rear leg and place it across your chest. Throw the kick out in an arc and snap the knee towards your opponent. Make contact with the heel. (Figs. 85 to 87)

Fig. 85

Fig. 86

Fig. 87

This kick can be used as a surprise ambush against a slow or predictable jab. The motion required to throw the kick actually takes you out of the path of the jab without additional actions, therefore it is fast in execution.

Its weakness lies in the fact that if you do not time it correctly, you are open to having your support leg 'swept' from under you.

The Spinning Hook Kick

Many people believe this kick to be even more powerful than the spinning backthrust kick. It is certainly strong and deserves the attention of the serious fighter.

The sequence is as follows: spin on your front foot. Bend your knee raising your leg close to your body. Throw the leg straight and continue spinning throughout the action. If your opponent blocks the technique, hook the kick around his guard. If he doesn't block keep the leg straight and rip it through with a strong hip action. (Figs. 88 to 90)

Use this kick sparingly and always as part of a combination. Although very strong, it requires a large body action and will be seen early unless you are careful.

Fig. 88

Fig. 89

Fig. 90

Jumping Kicks

Are jumping kicks effective? Many people would say no or at least that they are not worth the effort given their success rate. However I firmly believe that if you train correctly and above all use the jumping kicks at the right time, then they are superb weapons. As with so many large action techniques, timing is of the essence.

Here we will look at two jumping kicks. There are others, just as there are other normal kicks that have not been included, but it has to be said yet again that effectiveness is the goal, not the greatest possible range of techniques.

The Jumping Roundhouse Kick

The time to throw this technique is as your opponent retreats or when he momentarily stands still.

The moment of greatest danger is on the point of landing when you may be swept or countered heavily.

The sequence is as follows: jump high bringing both legs up. Twist your hips at the peak of the jump and throw a rear roundhouse kick at your opponent's head. Make contact with either the instep or shin. (Figs. 91 and 92)

Fig. 91

Fig. 92

Practise this technique on the big bag. Throw a combination of punches and let the momentum of your attack carry you forward. Add your jump to the momentum and release the kick.

A common mistake with this, and for that matter all other jumping kicks, is the desire to fire off the kick as soon as you are airborne. Keep in mind that your hips should be horizontally in line with the target when you make contact.

Fig. 93

Fig. 94

Fig. 95

The Jumping Backthrust Kick

The technique can be used either offensively or defensively. The targets are primarily the chest and stomach areas, although its effect should you connect with the head is devastating.

The offensive version is as follows: jump high and spin your body through 180 degrees. Ensure you turn your hips, shoulders and head. Drive your leg back straight. Make contact with the heel. (Figs. 93 to 95)

The defensive version is exactly the same as the offensive version except that your jump is backwards. It can be used close-in when fighting toe-to-toe with your opponent.

The sequence is as follows: push away from your opponent. Jump backwards and spin. Let the kick go at the peak of your jump. (Figs. 96 and 97)

The big bag and shield are the best pieces of equipment to develop this technique.

Fig. 96

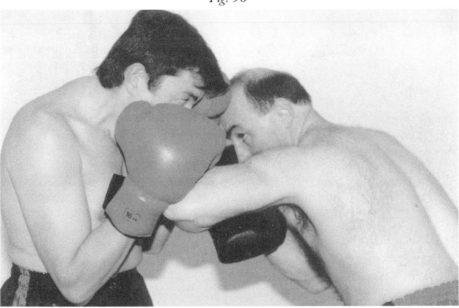

Fig. 97

Chapter Three:
Defence And Counter-Attack

'If he can't hit you he can't hurt you . . .
50 per cent of this game is not being hit.'
Geoff Britton

I started to train with Geoff Britton in the spring of 1979. At that point I was a fighter who tended to move into range and just unload.

For the first six months I don't believe I caught him 'clean' when sparring. He always seemed to read me, to counter me, especially as I started an attack. He appeared always to be outside my range, yet was able to hit me at will.

At last I had found a teacher who did not merely talk about body evasion, but lived it. His philosophy was simple . . . 'If he can't hit you he can't hurt you'.

The fighter must not confuse good defensive techniques with being negative. Rather they are a door through which you can launch telling counter-attacks.

Counter-attacking should always form part of a defensive move. Your aim must be to put a price on your opponent's aggression. This is the domain of the thinking fighter.

An opponent can be induced to attack so that he triggers your immediate and devastating response. This process can be likened to that of an insect blundering into the silken tripwires of a trapdoor spider . . .

The most common error in defence is overreaction and it is indicative of a nervous or inexperienced fighter.

Generally speaking, it is better to move rather than parry, parry rather than block and block rather than be hit.

Throughout the defence and counter your body must be relaxed; tension is the enemy of movement. You can only be relaxed if you have confidence in your defence. Later in this chapter we will examine a number of training methods which will exercise your defence and for the experienced fighter, keep it fine tuned.

It is perfectly possible to take a man off the streets and in a period of six months to a year of focus pad and bag work, teach him to deliver hard fast punches and kicks. Yet to avoid those very same techniques and to be able to counter effectively takes considerably longer. In fact it is common to see people climb into the ring with few or ineffective defensive techniques. The blame for this must lie squarely with the coach.

Slipping

Slipping is swaying to the side and slightly forward of a punch or kick. It may be performed to the outside or inside of a technique. Slipping to the outside is preferred because it is safer.

Slipping a Jab

The outside slip to a jab is performed by rolling the lead shoulder and taking a small forward step with your front foot, letting this action take your head to the outside of the punch. (Fig. 98)

Fig. 98

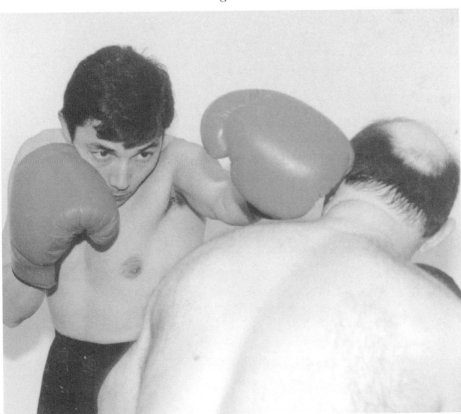

Fig. 99

From this position a left hook counter may be thrown to the chin (Fig. 99) or the body (Fig. 100).

Further counters are the lead jab to the short ribs, and a right uppercut from underneath the jab.

The inside slip to the jab is performed by rolling the right shoulder and letting the jab pass over it. (Fig. 101)

Warning: In this position you are open to your opponent's rear hand. Do not loiter.

Fig. 100

Fig. 101

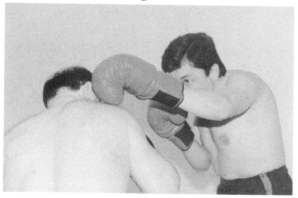

Fig. 102

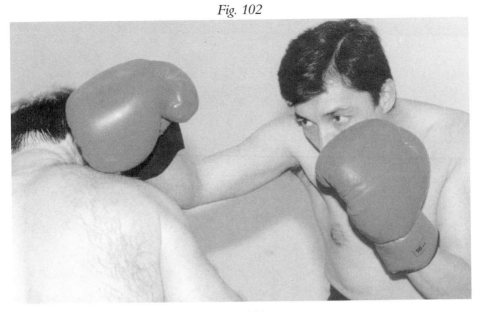

Fig. 103

Counters from this position are an overhand right, a left shovel hook to the solar plexus, a short right cross to the chin and a right cross to the ribs.

The outside slip to a right cross is performed by rolling the right shoulder and taking a small step forward with your lead foot, letting this action take your head to the outside of the punch. (Fig. 102)

Counters from this position are the right hook to the chin,
right cross to the liver (Fig. 103) and a right uppercut to the solar plexus.

The Layback

The layback calls for a fine appreciation of distance. When performed correctly it prepares the ground for a fast counter.

Fig. 104

The layback is performed by turning the rear foot slightly outwards and bending the knee (Fig. 104). This action moves your head back out of range, but leaves the feet in position and most importantly, flexes the back leg like a spring with which to power yourself forward.

Fig. 105

The layback may be employed against any and all attacks. The best counters to add to the layback are a fast snappy jab (Fig 105) and an over hand cross (Fig 106). The latter works because your opponent's return jab blinds him to the path of your counter.

Fig. 106

Fig. 107

Fig. 108

Fig. 109

Ducking

Ducking, as the name implies, is dropping below your opponent's attack (Fig. 107). The advantage of ducking is that it leaves both hands and both legs free to counter.

A strong counter may be launched from this position by using a spring hook or lead leg front kick (Fig. 108). Most powerful of all though is a rising rear uppercut, which when powered by the legs is devastating (Fig. 109).

When slipping, laying back or ducking, your aim should be to make your opponent miss by the merest fraction and to launch your counter-attack as soon as his attack has been nullified.

Practise these techniques as a set in front of the mirror - slip outside/slip inside/layback/duck. Keep your hands up in a full guard and observe your posture.

Next, have a partner throw four successive jabs at you and each time perform a different defence.

Lastly, move around having your partner throw different punches at you so that you build a sense of timing, throwing light counters at him as you do so.

Timing is vital when performing slips, laybacks or ducks. If you move too early your opponent will adjust his attack to compensate for your movement. If you move too late you will get hit.

Bobbing and Weaving

Bobbing and weaving link together slipping and ducking by way of a weaving motion (Figs. 110 to 112). Its purpose is to enable you to stay close to your opponent, countering heavily as you do so.

Fig. 110

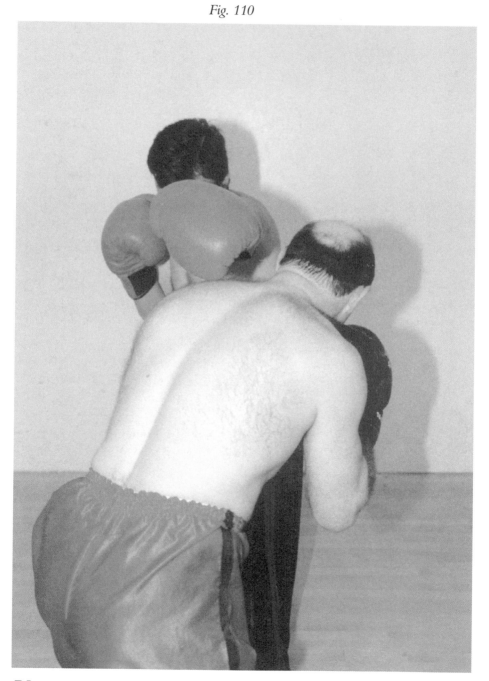

Fig. 111   *Fig. 112*

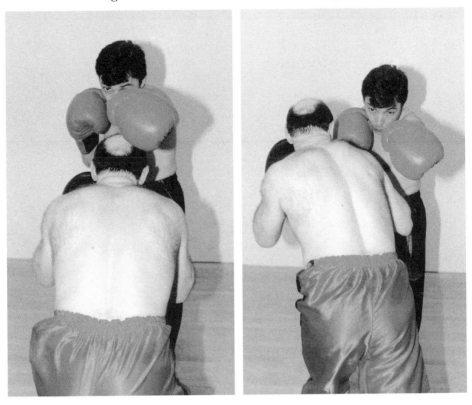

In order to practise this, stand toe-to-toe with a partner and have him throw half-speed jabs, crosses and hooks at you. Attempt to slip these and then weave from side to side. Have your partner gradually increase speed until you are able to deal with fast attacks.

This skill is a must for a short fighter whose opponent is attempting to keep him in range. It is the classic way of dealing with a fast accurate jab from a long-limbed opponent.

Bobbing and weaving on the edge of your opponent's reach will also tempt him into throwing techniques. When combined with good footwork (see 'Chapter Five: Timing, Distance and Mobility') it draws your opponent and opens up his guard.

Parrying

A parry is a light fast deflecting action performed with the hand.

The attacking limb when extended is like a lever, and only a small force at the end of a lever is necessary to deflect it.

To prove this, have a partner extend a jab towards you and then hold it fixed on your nose. With just two fingers of your rear hand push his fist to one side.

It is a rule of both parrying and blocking that they are performed close to the body. Never take your arms away from what they are trying to protect.

The Rear Hand Parry

The rear hand parry is a major defensive technique. It serves to absorb an attack by allowing your opponent to come close whilst at the same time leaving the front hand free to administer a sharp counter.

The rear hand parry against the jab is performed by steering away your opponent's jab with a sharp push against his wrist at the last possible moment (Fig. 113). Counter immediately with a lead hook to the chin or body.

The rear hand parry against a hook may be performed by first effecting a layback and applying the parry on your opponent's forearm. (Fig. 114)

Parries with the front hand are to be discouraged. Although possible they leave you open to strong rear hand counters. The exception is the lower parry.

Fig. 113

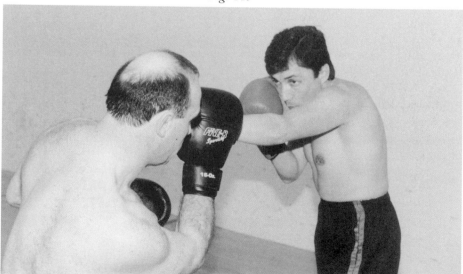

Fig. 114

The Lower Parry

The lower parry is used against kicks. As with all parries, its purpose is to deflect not block an attack.

The lower parry against a lead front or side kick. As your opponent kicks, drop your lead hand down and with a slapping motion deflect the attack to one side. Immediately counter with a strong cross. (Figs. 115 and 116)

Fig. 115

Fig. 116

Your opponent's foot should land across the mid-point line of his stance leaving him unbalanced and unable to follow up with further techniques. (Fig. 117)

Fig. 117

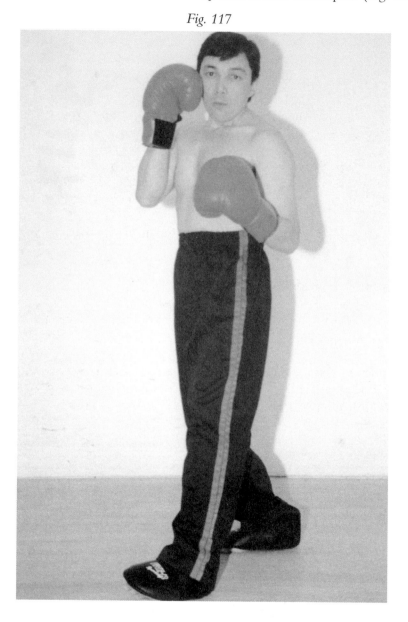

Care must be taken not to parry too forcefully, otherwise your opponent may use the parry as the trigger for a spinning backfist or one of the spinning kicks.

It has already been stated that parrying with the lead hand leaves you open, however because of the greater distance employed with a lower parry and the unbalancing effect on your opponent, it may be performed safely.

Blocking and Covering

Blocking is the action of opposing your opponent's attack by forcibly directing it away with either a hand, arm, shoulder or leg.

Covering is the action of using the arms and legs as a shield between you and your opponent's attack.

Blocks and covers are employed when movement is not possible and parrying is too dangerous.

It should be noted that taking too many blows on the arms, particularly kicks, weakens them and may result in you having to lower them. This will expose your head to attack and is the main reason why movement and parrying are preferred.

Many Thai boxers kick with their shins into the upper arm to achieve precisely this.

The Shoulder Raise

The shoulder raise is a simple and economical method of blocking either a cross or a rear roundhouse kick.

The shoulder raise as a block against a cross: as your opponent throws a cross, raise your lead shoulder and let the glove 'bounce' off the shoulder's rounded edge (Fig. 118). You may assist the raise by a slight layback.

Fig. 118

The shoulder raise against a rear roundhouse is performed as follows: raise your lead shoulder and take a small pace sideways with your rear foot. At the same time angle your body away from the force of the kick. All three actions performed simultaneously will negate the force of the strongest rear roundhouse. (Fig. 119)

Fig. 119

Build confidence by having a partner throw crosses and roundhouse kicks at you slowly. Work up to maximum speed and power. Once you can effect and therefore trust this technique, you will find it invaluable.

The Forearm Block

The forearm block is performed as follows: as your opponent throws a cross raise your lead elbow (not your glove) and using the middle of your forearm, direct the cross upwards. (Fig. 120)

Fig. 120

A sharp snappy motion is required rather than a forceful push. The degree of displacement of your opponent's punch is considerable - due once again to the leverage principle. Take care not to overcommit on the forearm block, otherwise you will expose your ribs to follow up blows.

The Catch

The catch is a block performed with the rear hand against either a jab or a cross.

The catch against the jab is performed as follows: as your opponent throws the jab, open your rear hand and catch his glove like a ball. Immediately fire a jab as a counter. (Figs. 121 and 122)

Fig. 121

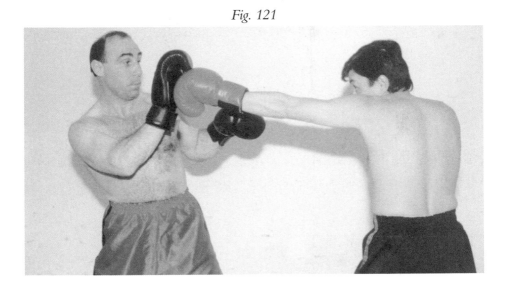

Fig. 122

Be careful not to reach too far forward with the catching hand, otherwise you will set yourself up for a left hook.

The catch may also be turned into a 'meet' by taking a step to the side with your lead leg and throwing the jab counter at the same time as you catch his punch. (Fig. 123)

The catch against the cross is performed exactly as above, although you must take some account of the additional power behind the technique by taking a small step backwards to absorb the worst of it.

To practise the catch and return, work with a partner and a focus pad. Get him to throw jabs at your face, catch them and return your own jabs, aiming at his focus pad. (Fig. 124)

With practice this becomes a fast, economical counter which will inhibit his desire to lead.

Fig. 123

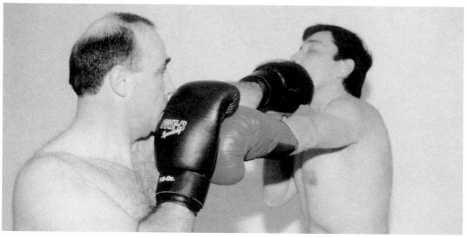

Fig. 124

The Leg Block

The leg block is used against kicks and primarily roundhouse kicks.

The sequence for throwing a leg block is as follows: as your opponent throws a roundhouse kick, lift up your lead leg and absorb the kick across your lower and upper legs. This block may be combined with an arm block by bringing your arm fractionally down to meet your leg. (Fig. 125)

This protects the entire side of your body and head and is an excellent way of defending against a strong opponent.

Fig. 125

Covering

As stated above, covering is using your legs and arms as shields to keep attacks off the target areas. (Fig. 126 and 127)

A poor technician will cover out of desperation and should be punished with attacks around the edge and through the middle of his cover.

If you are forced on the defensive, particularly against the ropes or in a corner and have to cover, then you should aim to grab and turn your opponent (Figs. 128 and 129). A strong opponent who resists being turned must first be swept to dislodge his balance.

*

It is a fact that under pressure fighters move away from the threat of being hit. However, it is far easier for your opponent to move forward throwing techniques than for you to move backwards defending against them. In order for you to be successful in defence therefore, you must always seek to use a proper defensive technique and then counter immediately.

Fig. 126

Fig. 127

Fig. 128

Fig. 129

Training Methods

There are specialised forms of sparring that force you to exercise your defence without the option of running away.

Warning: Care should always be taken to ensure sparring is controlled.

Both the methods used here should be performed under the supervision of a coach.

Sparring on the Wall

Take up a full guard and stand with your rear foot against a wall. Have your partner throw punches at normal speed, but with reduced power. Rock and roll your body as you absorb his attacks on your gloves, forearms, elbows and shoulders, seizing every opportunity to apply a slip, duck, layback, parry or block together with suitable counters. (Fig. 130)

At first you will tense up and get hit everywhere, but with practice you will learn to treat each attack on its merits. Remember tension is your enemy, not the man in front of you.

Later, experiment with the half guard and the cross guard.

Finally, throw the legs into the equation! (Fig. 131)

I strongly recommend this practice method to all fighters as it will find the gaps in your defence quicker than anything else. It also forces you to counter, if only to keep your partner at bay.

Fig. 130   *Fig. 131*

Tied Sparring

Warning: This is an advanced form of training and should only be attempted by more experienced fighters.

Take two martial arts belts (you can substitute a rope) and tie them together. Now have your partner tie one end around his waist whilst you tie the other around yours. The gap between you should be approximately four feet.

Now spar normally. (Fig. 132)

The imposed fighting range forces you to continually think about defence as well as attack. It allows you slightly greater freedom of movement than the 'on the wall' method, whilst retaining the function of exercising your defence.

Fig. 132

Mobile Defence

The most instinctive of defensive techniques is mobility. The action of running away does not have to be taught(!)

For the fighter however, unthinking movement will lead to disaster. All defensive footwork, whether forward, backward or sideways, should serve a purpose and once again it has to be said that the purpose is counter-attack.

The sequence that should be memorised is: movement, hit, movement.

A fighter should never be stationary and footwork should be used constructively. (See 'Chapter Five: Timing, Distance and Mobility')

Clumsy footwork comes from not understanding the basics.

1) It is essential that a fighter maintains his balance at all times.

2) In order to evade an attack, you must push away with the foot nearest to the threat. i.e. If you are standing in front of your opponent and he throws a straight punch or kick, you push with your lead foot, thus carrying your body backwards. Equally, if he throws a hook punch or roundhouse kick, you push away with the foot on that side.

3) Move only sufficiently to enable you to evade the hit or to dissipate its energy to the point where it cannot hurt you.

4) As soon as you are safe, launch a strong counter-attack.

5) Continue attacking if you have hurt him or move out of range of his retaliation.

Selected Evasions and Counters

Against a jab: push strongly away from your opponent's jab with your lead foot. As his attack misses, push strongly off your rear foot and throw either a jab or lead leg front kick counter.

Against a cross: sidestep to your left by pushing strongly off your rear foot. Throw a rear roundhouse kick across your opponent's body.

Against a backthrust kick: step forward at 45 degrees, pushing off your rear foot. Throw a strong right hook to your opponent's head. (Fig. 133)

These are just some of the many defences and counters possible using defensive footwork. Experiment using different techniques until you have solutions to the most common attacks.

Movement is superior to all other forms of defence and along with distance and timing, forms the bedrock of the successful fighter.

Fig. 133

Summary

Step by step you must learn the techniques of defence. They are the individual bricks in the wall that will protect you.

It must always be borne in mind that a fighter who is connecting with the target area is a confident aggressive fighter. Equally, a fighter who is missing loses confidence, loses trust in the very techniques he needs to win.

To make an opponent miss is to attack the very root of his skill, his decision-making process. If to this you add punishing counters, then his defeat is only a question of time.

Chapter Four: Combinations

The purpose of a combination is to break down your opponent's defence by means of a series of techniques that search out or create gaps in his guard.

There is no guard that an opponent can offer that makes him totally safe, and close observation should reveal areas of weakness.

Ideally, a combination should force your opponent to start committing with large blocking motions that leave holes in his defence. If you manage to achieve this, you should capitalise quickly by driving in with heavy techniques.

Typical combinations are a mix of straight, round, rising and spinning techniques aimed at both the body and the head. Within these techniques should be feints and time intervals (see 'Chapter Five: Timing, Distance and Mobility') that draw your opponent out and leave him vulnerable to particular techniques.

Combinations fall into two categories, offensive and defensive. An offensive combination should start with a fast technique that does not commit you immediately. Remember at all times that your opponent may be waiting for you so that he can launch a telling counter-attack.

Both jabs and lead leg front kicks are good openers. They disturb your own guard the least and can quickly be followed up by the more powerful rear hand and leg techniques.

Offensive Combinations

Double Jab

The simplest and one of the most effective combinations is the double jab. The term 'simple' here refers to the most economical in terms of body mechanics.

This combination works because most people instinctively move away from an attack. By doubling up the jab you catch your opponent on the back foot with the second jab and thus unable to effectively counter you.

The variety and subtlety attainable with this combination is endless. The first variant is a double jab to the head (Figs. 134 and 135). It should be used frequently in order to keep your opponent on the defensive, both mentally and physically.

The second variant is a jab to the head followed by a jab to the body. Again, instinct will make the unsophisticated fighter raise his hands to block the head jab, leaving his body open. Drive in deep with the body jab, keeping your arm stiff at the moment of impact.

The third variant comprises a body jab followed by a head jab. The fourth, a feint to the body followed by a double head jab. Now add angled, rising and dropping jabs (see 'Chapter One: Fundamentals') plus feints. Variety creates havoc with an opponent's defences.

Work with the focus pads until you can fire in hard fast double jabs with plenty of sting. Lastly, the double jab can itself be the start of a more punishing combination.

Fig. 134

Fig. 135

Jab/Cross

The jab/cross combination is the perfect blend of speed and power. It should form part of every fighter's arsenal. Practise it on both the bag and the focus pads until you can throw it smoothly with real venom.

The simplest form of this combination is the jab to the head followed by the cross to the head (Figs. 136 and 137). Remember to move your rear foot in half a step as you cross, so as to put your body weight into the punch.

Fig. 136

Fig. 137

A superb variant of the above is the fast jab to the body followed by an overhand cross to the head, especially against an opponent who overreacts against the jab. (Figs. 138 and 139)

Another variant is the double jab followed by a cross to the head. Frequently, when an opponent is going backwards under pressure, (e.g. from a double jab) his defences are weak. At this moment a strong cross will catch him by blasting straight between his arms.

Fig. 138

Fig. 139

Jab/Hook

The jab/hook combination aims to draw your opponent into blocking the straight jab and thereby sets him up for the hook to come around his guard. (Figs. 140 and 141)

This is a 'tester' for your opponent because it forces him to move his guard and leaves him open for other shots. It is made for the opponent who habitually 'catches' your jabs and makes his rear 'catching hand' come too far forward. Use it frequently and occasionally reverse the combination – throw the hook and induce him to bring out his rear arm to cover it, then shoot a jab into the gap created. (Figs. 142 and 143)

Another variant of this combination is the jab to the body followed by the left hook to the head – the jab could be a feint that allows a stinging hook to land cleanly.

Remember, combinations that vary both the target and path of attack (e.g. body/straight punch and then head/round punch) are very effective.

Fig. 140   *Fig. 141*

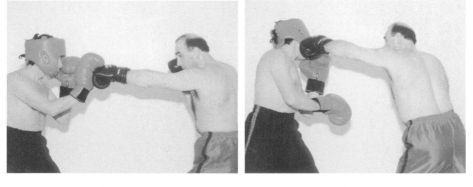

Fig. 142   *Fig. 143*

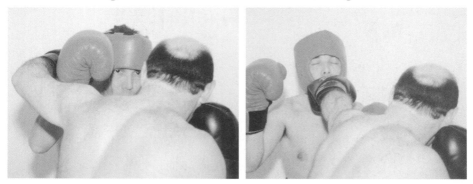

Jab/Cross/Hook

This combination combines speed, power and deceptiveness. Throw the jab fast, power in the cross and then whip the hook behind his guarding hand and on to his chin before he has time to react.
(Figs. 144 to 146)

A subtle skill here is to place the smallest possible 'time interval' (pause) between the cross and the hook. This enables you to perceive whether your opponent covers his head against the hook. If he does, throw it to the body.

A further variation is the jab/cross/shovel hook. This works very well when your opponent covers his head at the slightest aggression.

Remember to twist your ankle, hip and shoulder behind the shovel hook.

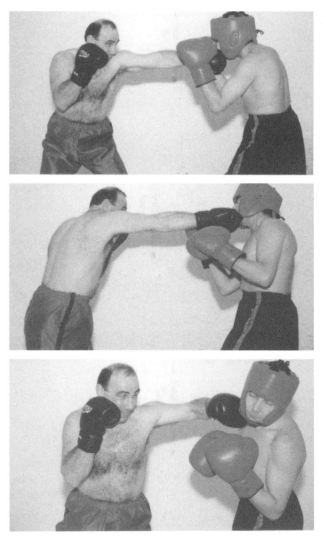

Fig. 144

Fig. 145

Fig. 146

Lead Body Hook/Lead Head Hook

This powerful combination should only be thrown as part of a larger combination or when you have 'timed' your opponent.

It works particularly well when you have backed an opponent into a corner or against the ropes and he attempts to cover up.

Lean slightly to your left and throw a hard lead body hook into your opponent's liver (this is located half under and half on the lower ribs of you opponent's right side - see the Appendix: Targets and Techniques). This should make your opponent drop his elbow to cover the shot, (few people can take two liver shots!) then pivot fast and throw a lead hook to the chin.
(Figs. 147 and 148)

If your opponent carries his guard wide, throw the body hook into his solar plexus and then the chin.

Curve you body behind the shots to add power. A cross can be added to the combination to finish your opponent. Practise this on the focus pads and feel the power.

Fig. 147

Fig. 148

Jab/Cross/Shovel Hook/Overhand Right

A very strong combination that can turn a fight. It has all the elements of the superior attack, using straight/round/body and head shots.

Throw a fast jab/cross to the head, then pivot strongly and drive in a shovel hook to the solar plexus, finish with a strong overhand right cross.
(Figs. 149 to 152)

Aim to make the techniques flow and pivot your body behind the punches to add extra power. Keep yourself loose so that the punches obtain maximum speed.

Lastly, a lead hook to the chin may be added to the combination to help re-close your guard.

Fig. 149   *Fig. 150*

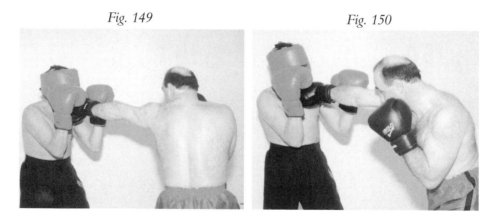

Fig. 151   *Fig. 152*

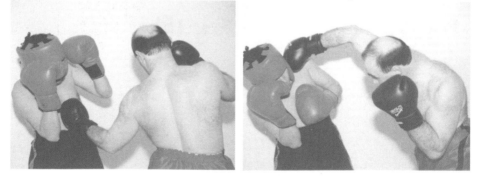

Rear Uppercut/Lead Hook to Chin

Hooks and uppercuts work very well in combination. One frequently sets up the other. They are good tools for opening up a tight guard, for example when your opponent is trapped on the ropes or in a corner.

Only use an uppercut to lead if your opponent is covering whilst under pressure or as an opportunistic counter.

Throw a rear uppercut with strong ankle and hip rotation, (do not swing the arm) the punch should come between your opponent's arms, now throw the lead hook and strike his exposed chin. (Figs. 153 and 154)

Fig. 153

Fig. 154

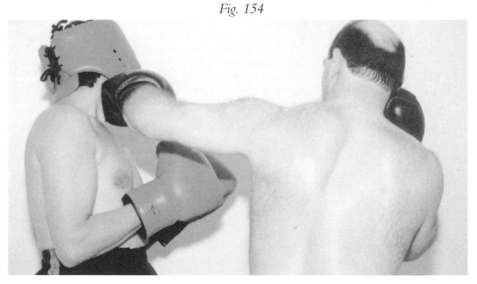

A right cross can be added as a finishing blow.

You must watch your opponent's reactions throughout a combination and be ready to switch targets and techniques as and when the opportunity arises.

With craft it is possible to lure or pressure your opponent on to your favourite technique or combination.

When combining hands and legs it is generally more effective to kick from the same side as the last punch i.e. left punch/right punch/right kick or left punch/right punch/left punch/left kick.

This makes the combination flow more easily and prevents large body movements which expose your target areas to the opponent.

Like any rule there are exceptions, but the gain must always be weighed against the potential loss.

The first two hand/leg combinations shown are the simplest and therefore most effective combinations using this principle.

Jab/Lead Roundhouse Kick to the Body

It has been mentioned before, but bears repeating because of its importance: when combining hand and leg techniques, you must ensure that your legs follow the hands unless you are an exceptional kicker.

This combination of jab/lead roundhouse to the body is a fast and economical combination that has a high success rate.

Throw the jab and then fire in the lead leg roundhouse kick just under his right elbow, twisting sharply on your support leg and snapping your knee.
(Figs. 155 and 156)

Fig. 155   *Fig. 156*

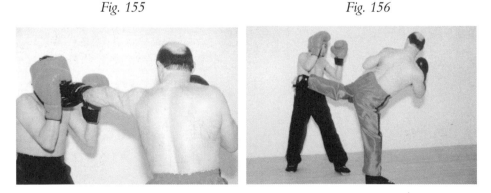

This combination can be used as a 'pot-boiler' to keep pushing up your tally of points, also, because of its economy, it is the perfect combination to throw early on in the fight when you are unsure of your opponent's ability.

Jab/Cross/Rear Roundhouse Kick to the Body

We have already stated in Chapter One that the rear roundhouse kick is the Exocet missile of kick boxing. This combination enables you to make full use of a strong roundhouse and therefore should be practised until it is second nature.

Throw the jab to the chin and follow quickly with a deep penetrating cross, then slam the rear roundhouse in under your opponent's left elbow.
(Figs. 157 to 159)

Variants of this combination use the sidestep roundhouse and the body shift roundhouse for extra power - mix them up and keep your opponent guessing.

Use the big bag to hone this combination.

Fig. 157

Fig. 158

Fig. 159

Double Jab/Backthrust Kick to the Body

It is important that when using any spinning technique you first set it up. This combination ensures that your opponent is on the back foot, and therefore unable to effectively counter you, before you throw the kick.

Throw the double jab to the face with lots of speed and snap to get your opponent retreating. Then spin fast, turning your head and shoulders ahead of the kick before driving home the backthrust to the stomach.
(Figs. 160 and 161)

If your opponent has a tendency to let his guard widen when retreating under pressure, then the backthrust kick can be thrown to the head.

Fig. 160

Fig. 161

Jab/Spinning Backfist/Rear Roundhouse Kick to the Body

This is an unorthodox combination that works surprisingly well. The rear roundhouse kick is especially effective because of the additional reach it lends.

Throw the jab and immediately spin into the backfist before your opponent can recover. Then turn sharply on your support leg and power in the rear roundhouse kick with plenty of hip. (Figs. 162 to 164)

Fig. 162

Fig. 163

Fig. 164

Practise the combination in the air and then progress to focus pads. As you master the spin you will be able to add more and more power to the kick. Obviously this is not a bread and butter combination. Use it sparingly to ambush your opponent.

A subtle way of beginning this combination is to make the jab a feint and spin straight into the backfist. If you choose this method, make sure the feint crosses your opponent's line of sight or he may hit you with a heavy counter.

Jab/Cross/Footsweep/Lead Roundhouse to Body

Sweeps in combinations are used not as much to down an opponent as to pin his weight on his rear leg, thus making it impossible for him to move away from your follow up techniques.

Throw the jab/cross fast and then sweep his lead leg with a rear footsweep. Immediately follow up with a lead leg roundhouse to his midsection before he can regain his balance.
(Figs. 165 to 168)

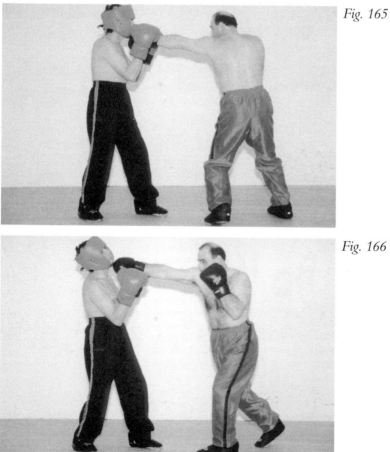

Fig. 165

Fig. 166

Fig. 167

Fig. 168

A cross may be added to finish him off.

Sweeps can be inserted into any number of combinations. They are an effective way of creating doubt in an opponent's mind.

Left Hook/Spinning Hook Kick

There are many opportunities to lead with a hook. Most depend on timing or your opponent dropping his rear guard hand when jabbing, thus exposing his chin.

Throw the lead hook as normal, but continue to turn. Pivot your head, shoulders and hips and then throw the spinning hook kick.
(Figs. 169 and 170)

A front kick to the body can be added as insurance against your opponent lunging in when the spinning hook kick has passed.

Fig. 169

Fig. 170

Lead Side Kick/Lead Hook

This is one of the few occasions when leading with the leg actually gains an advantage. The path of the kick forces your opponent to bring his arms down to keep the kick away from his ribs. Begin the combination from a half guard/straddle stance. Get to this position using a series of small movements disguised by feints and actual techniques. It is a mistake to suddenly change from a full guard/basic stance as this telegraphs your intention. Step in fast and throw the side kick hard at your opponent's ribs. As he reacts, pivot strongly over your lead foot and whip the hook on to his chin (Figs. 171 and 172). A feint jab to the face may be used initially in order to make your opponent raise his arms, thus opening up the ribs to be kicked.

Fig. 171

Fig. 172

Jab/Hook/Jump Backthrust Kick

The jab/hook combination should be done in order to get your opponent to raise his hands. As soon as he does so, jump and spin into the backthrust kick.(Figs. 173 to 175)

Be prepared to continue with further techniques on landing as it is at this point that you are most vulnerable.

Fig. 173

Fig. 174

Fig. 175

Jab/Cross/Jumping Roundhouse Kick

The key to this combination is flow. Let the jab/cross carry your body forward. Add the jump to this forward momentum and let the kick go at the top of the jump. (Figs. 176 to 178)

There can be nothing halfhearted about a jumping kick. If you do not possess the skill and confidence to fully commit behind the technique, you have no business throwing it.

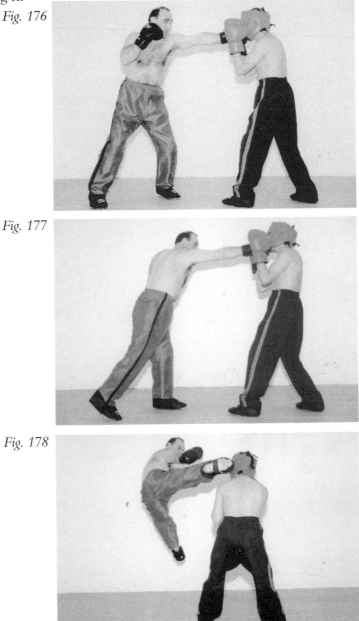

Fig. 176

Fig. 177

Fig. 178

Jab/Lead Hook Kick to the Head

Hook kicks are notoriously difficult to read once underway. Therefore, if you make the jab a fast 'blinder' that engages your opponent's full attention, he will not see the kick until it is too late. Also use the jab to cover your step up. (Figs. 179 and 180)

Remember to mix up the combination by using some or all of the suggested variations to keep your opponent guessing. If he starts to 'read' you, you will get countered by a defensive combination.

Fig. 179

Fig. 180

Defensive Combinations

These are combinations starting with a 'meet' and are therefore triggered by your opponent's attack. They are representative of the most aggressive form of fighting as they deny your opponent the opportunity of respite.

The key things to look for when using defensive combinations are gaps created in a opponent's guard due to the execution of his attack. Below are listed some of the most common errors in attacking technique which should instantly be met with a forceful defensive combination.

1) When executing a jab your opponent fails to return his lead hand to the correct guard. 'Meet' the jab with an overhand cross and lead hook to the chin.

2) When executing a jab your opponent scissors his rear guard hand, thus exposing his chin (Fig. 181). 'Meet' with a spinning hook kick and left front kick combination. Continue with a cross/hook.

3) When throwing a cross your opponent fails to move his rear foot in behind the technique. 'Meet' by executing a spinning backthrust kick to the liver followed by a cross.

4) Your opponent leads with a cross without timing it. 'Meet' it with a snapping lead front kick to the body, followed by a sidestep roundhouse to the ribs.

5) When your opponent throws a rear leg roundhouse he fails to keep his guard tight. 'Meet' it with a left arm cover (Fig. 182) and a cross to the solar plexus followed by a body hook/head hook combination.

6) When your opponent throws a lead leg roundhouse kick, he again fails to keep his guard tight. 'Meet' it with a right arm cover (Fig. 183) and a lead hook to the body followed by an overhand cross to the chin.

Fig. 181   *Fig. 182*   *Fig. 183*

Defensive combinations used against sweeps have the additional advantage of using your opponent's sweep power in your own counter. Further, whilst sweeping, your opponent is standing on one leg and therefore unable to move away from the defensive combination that follows. Below are some examples.

1) As your opponent sweeps, go with the turning action and 'meet' him with a spinning backfist followed by a cross. (Figs. 184 and 185)

2) As your opponent sweeps, you let the energy of the sweep pick up your foot. 'Meet' him with a lead hook kick, (Fig. 186) and then a cross.

Fig. 184

Fig. 185

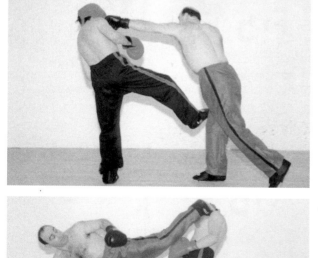

Fig. 186

3)   As your opponent sweeps you, let the energy pick up your foot and 'meet' him with a lead side kick followed by a rear roundhouse to the head. (Figs. 187 and 188)

Fig. 187

Fig. 188

Practise these techniques by having a partner sweep you gently. Let your leg rise or turn and 'meet' him with whatever feels most natural. Timing is a crucial element here.

Have your partner increase the speed and power of his sweep until you can instantly counter him.

*

It should be remembered that flow is as important as speed and power to a combination. Shadow-boxing is the means to obtain flow.

You should pivot and curve your body behind the techniques in order to maximise their power. Arm and leg power alone are insufficient.

Note all errors in your opponent's attacking techniques and make him pay for them by applying a defensive combination.

Chapter Five:
Timing, Distance and Mobility

Timing and distance considerations will occupy three quarters of a trained fighter's mental activity and good footwork or mobility, is what controls timing and distance.

It is an oft used cliché that boxing and kick boxing are games of chess, but cliché or not, the intelligent fighter must always be a calculating fighter, and timing, distance and mobility are the keys to unlock an opponent.

Timing

'When the strike of the hawk breaks the body of its prey, it is because of timing.'
Sun Tzu - **The Art of War**

Timing can be defined as the ability to pick the precise moment to attack, move or defend. The calculation of 'when' is based on a thousand tiny pieces of information. Anticipation, reaction, observation and experience, will all play a role in choosing this moment.

Hesitation is the enemy of timing. Hesitation is caused by ring rust, fatigue, lack of confidence, under training and inexperience.

So subtle is the art of timing that the best fighters are frequently unaware of any precise calculation, they just do it. This is because there is no longer a gap between their thinking and acting. In Japanese swordsmanship there is an apt saying: 'Did I move the sword or did the sword move me?'

This does not mean that you should not think, just that at the highest level of training thinking and acting are both simultaneous and instant.

There are two halves to timing - what you are doing and what your opponent is doing. To launch an attack without timing is to invite disaster.

Application of Timing

Your opponent will be open to attack if he telegraphs his intention. This telegraphing or as it is sometimes called 'loading up', requires an immediate response, a fast jab or lead leg front kick as a stop-hit to throw out his attack.

Alternatively you can ambush him by launching a defensive combination at the very moment of his attack.

If your opponent continually telegraphs his intent then you should 'give' him openings and punish his attempts to take them.

If a fight is long, hard or difficult your opponent may lose concentration momentarily. This mental inertia is the perfect opportunity for you to launch a heavy combination.

Complaining to the referee, looking back at his cornermen and particular facial expressions, such as disgust, anger or mock humour, are all indications that he is not concentrating on the job in hand.

Loss of balance is also an opportunity to attack. This may be accidental on your opponent's part or it may be deliberately brought about by you as a result of pressure or perhaps a sweep.

Hesitation by your opponent can occur for all sorts of reasons and should be treated the same as lack of concentration. Punish it quickly.

Signs of fatigue are also an opportunity for you to attack. Fatigue manifests itself in many ways, from obvious difficulty in breathing through to an unwillingness to launch an attack or adequate defence.

On noticing fatigue you should aim to add to your opponent's difficulties by unrelenting body shots with both punches and kicks. Tired fighters defend badly. If he overreacts by covering his body, switch to the head and then back to the body again.

Feinting is the tool with which to check that the moment is right to attack.

Feinting should draw a response from your opponent such as movement or the launch of a counter. Feints can also be used at any time during a combination in order to 'throw out' your opponent's defensive timing.

Feints work best when you have hurt an opponent with a particular technique, for example having hit your opponent with a strong lead hook to the chin, you immediately throw another as a feint and when your opponent defends by covering his head you switch to a body hook.

Feints should always engage an opponent's attention. The degree of movement by you during a feint depends on any number of factors, but chief among them is the tendency of your opponent to overreact.

Distance

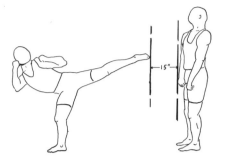

Diagram 1

'Add a step to it!'
A Spartan mother's reply to her son who complained that his sword was short compared to the Persians'.

Distance is determined in the first instance by your opponent's reach. Normally, this is his furthest reach plus half a step (to enable you to 'time' him).
(Diagram 1)

This 'reach distance' should be thought of as an imaginary line that runs between you and your opponent. (Diagram 2) Another way of thinking of it is as a segment of a circle, with your opponent at the circle's centre and the arc of the circumference as the danger mark for yourself. (Diagram 3)

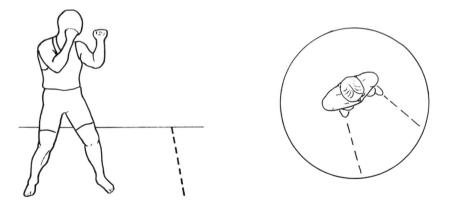

Diagram 2   *Diagram 3*

You should constantly move forwards and backwards across this line in order to agitate your opponent and cause him to misjudge the distance and fire off his attack either too soon or too late.

Although 'reach distance' is the norm, other factors can also play a part in determining where you should be in relation to your opponent.

1) The speed of his attack may be such that 'reach distance' is insufficient. In order to be safe you should be able to defend, move or counter from a position of safety. The faster he is the greater the distance may have to be.

2) The penetration of his attack (distance covered) may be so great that you need additional space. The reverse of this is that he may need space to launch an attack, and you should of course deny him this.

These three variables, reach distance, speed distance and penetration distance apply as much to your own attacks as to your opponent's. But whatever the variables, it must be you that controls the distance.

The most obvious example of this is a tall man fighting a short powerful man. Each, for his own reasons, wants the distance to be different.

The tall man wants his opponent on the end of his long weapons where he can hit him and also deny him the chance of striking back. The short powerful man wants to be on the inside where he can make his power tell and where the long limbs of the tall man are a disadvantage. Whoever achieves his personally preferred distance the most will be the winner.

Another example is that at the beginning of a fight you may choose to be cautious until you have learnt about your opponent, therefore you will want additional range, but as the fight progresses you may wish to shorten the distance in order to land more telling blows.

In a long fight the man dictating events may change, these periods of ascendancy will of course affect distance. In the closing stages of a fight, if one man is the stronger then the distance will be inches as he drives home the finishing punches and kicks.

It is essential that your training takes in sparring at various distances in order to meet changing fortunes.

Fine distance appreciation is called for in order to remain within effective countering distance. Try to keep within countering range by using angular retreat, circling and by swaying, ducking, bobbing and weaving.

Fast variable tools such as the jab and the lead leg front kick are recommended to test distance and also an opponent's awareness.

Distance and timing are but two sides of the same coin. An appreciation of both is required for effective fighting.

The changing of distance and the timing of an attack are dependent on mobility.

Mobility

Mobility is movement. Planned, structured movement that places your opponent at a disadvantage and you in a position of dominance.

There are two halves to mobility. Footwork and upper body movement. These two are not mutually exclusive, and they can accomplish different tasks at the same time.

For example your feet may be propelling you forward into range so as to launch an attack, but at the same time your upper body will be ducking and swaying in order to get your opponent to counter too soon, thus your feet are achieving distance and your upper body timing.

Footwork

Footwork consists of stepping, sliding and lunging. These are the ABC of mobility.

Conversely, inertia is the opposite of movement. Inertia can be defined as the state of rest or immobility. In order for you to move, you must overcome inertia and footwork is what creates movement.

Mobility is dependant on the effective maintenance of your balance. Controlled footwork is essential. Therefore at all times you must keep movement as relaxed and natural as possible. If it's awkward then it may provide your opponent with an opening. Clearly, in order to move freely you must be mentally relaxed.

Large movements may mean a delay in defence or attack, as the larger the movement, the greater the disturbance to your balance.

Small movements that use speed and subtlety are the goal. Unnecessary movement is a drain on your energy bank.

There is a tendency for fighters to increase their evasive movements according to the strength of an opponent's attack. This is wrong. If you make him miss you achieve the same success whether it is by inches or feet.

Mobility is the experienced fighter's chosen method of defence.

Stepping

Stepping in a fighting context means simply taking a pace in order to advance, retreat or evade.

As you move you should allow your body to adjust the length of pace, and your balance naturally. However, against this your opponent will try to out-pace you and catch you flatfooted.

To all intents and purposes, flatfootedness and inertia are the same. Momentary loss of the ability to move. The means to overcome this is the small explosive step.

The Small Explosive Step

Both inertia and attempted large movements cost you time and it is precisely time that your opponent needs to complete his attack.

The small explosive step is a step of no more than four inches that carries your body either to the left, right, forward or back. Although primarily defensive, it can be used to set up a counter.

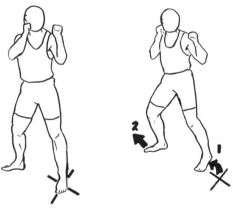

Diagram 4   *Diagram 5*

The foot nearest to the threat is lifted and stabbed into the floor no more than four inches from its original position. As soon as the foot lands, push off again in the same direction. (Diagram 4 and 5)

This explosive movement acts to overcome inertia with rapid movement, which is then reinforced by the second step. The speed of the step propels you to safety.

The Step-Up

The step-up is a half step performed by the back leg. The rear foot is placed speedily behind the front foot and then pushes off, propelling the body forward.

An obvious example of this is the lead leg front kick. (See Chapter One.)

The beauty of this step is that a jab can be used during the step-up phase thus 'blinding' your opponent to your movement.

Sliding

Sliding is a smooth movement that minimises the raising of the foot. Lift the front foot and transfer your weight forward, ensuring that your lead foot skims the ground. (Diagrams 6 to 8)

Sliding is one of the two preferred ways of moving when attacking, the other being lunging. In terms of energy expenditure it is the most economical. Sliding and jabbing are co-dependent and should be practised together.

Diagrams 6, 7 and 8

Lunging

Lunging is a fast forward commitment of the lead leg towards your opponent.

Pick up your lead foot and drive strongly off the rear foot. It is important to have your rear heel off the floor so that the foot is in the correct position for pushing. (Diagram 9)

When lunging with a kick, make sure your foot moves before your body, otherwise you will telegraph your intent. Pick up the lead foot and lunge into the kick. (Diagram 10 and 11)

You can lunge with lead front, roundhouse or side kicks. Lunging is best performed when chasing an opponent.

Diagram 9

Diagrams 10 and 11

Rhythmic/Arrhythmic Movement

Rhythmic movement is the essence of economy. Providing you are in control of the fight, rhythmic movement will aid energy conservation and the flow of techniques. However, because of it's nature it gives your opponent an opportunity to 'time' you.

Arrhythmic movement is a series of staccato steps that are seemingly random and almost impossible to 'time'. Use it in both attack and defence. In attack it can be used during a combination to thwart your opponent's defences.

It can be likened to putting your foot on a car's accelerator and taking it off at irregular intervals. This stop/go is high in energy expenditure and should only be used in short bursts of action.

In defence it varies your evasion techniques and wrong foots your attacker.

Timing in movement is really a question of mixing rhythmic and arrhythmic movements in order to gain an advantage.

Time Interval

A time interval or pause is a deliberate gap in the flow of a combination or series of movements. It is akin to arrhythmic movement except that it momentarily 'freezes' your actions.

There are many variations on the theme, but they all come down to one thing, throwing out your opponent's timing.

Upper Body Mobility

Upper body mobility uses movement to prevent your opponent lining up a target and scoring on it.

Slipping, ducking, layback, bobbing and weaving, shoulder rolling and rotating the trunk are all methods of making it difficult for your opponent to hit you cleanly.

All these methods are explained in 'Chapter Three: Defence and Counter-Attack'. The difference here is that they are not applied in order to effect a particular defence, but rather to prevent your opponent being able to attack effectively.

Together with good footwork, upper body mobility will reduce your opponent's number of effective scoring techniques throughout the course of the fight.

Ring Mobility

Mobility in relation to the ring is an area that must be studied by the fighter. It is a specialised field because there is little comparison between fighting in a ring and out of it.

In an open, unrestricted area, such as a gym, a fighter under pressure can continually retreat. Within the confines of a ring however, a fighter who retreats in a straight line will quickly find himself against the ropes or in a corner.

Equally, the dimensions of a ring affect mobility. A fighter who appreciates both aspects, confinement and dimension, can dominate a contest.

An oft used tactic whilst fighting is to gain and maintain the centre of the ring. At first this sounds like immobility, but it should be recognised that true mobility is not about large unstructured movement, rather, it is about moving just enough.

Rings vary in size. Broadly speaking you should aim to dominate the middle four square feet. This is plenty of room in which to apply your tactics and techniques. (Diagram 12)

Your opponent however will have to circle the outside of the ring, expending valuable energy as he does so. (Diagram 13)

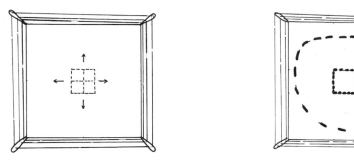

Diagram 12   Diagram 13

Considerable time and effort may be spent in acquiring and holding on to the centre of the ring. The number of movements and counter-movements necessary for this are usually determined by how equal the fighters are.

If both fighters are matched in technique, power and stamina, then the whole contest may quite literary 'revolve' around the centre of the ring.

The reverse of dominating the centre of the ring is continual evasion. Many fighters use this strategy and it is termed 'hit and run'.

Usually the fighter who 'hits and runs' is not a powerful hitter and has chosen this method of fighting so as not to get drawn into a war.

He will move just ahead of his opponent and punish him as he chases. If the chasing fighter loses patience and charges in blindly, then he will be met by stinging techniques or a fast sidestep that will rob him of confidence and leave him open to further counters.

A fighter who displays skill in 'hit and run' must be cut off and punished hard to the body. This is achieved by using counter-movements that force your opponent into weak positions such as on the ropes or in the corner, where his superior mobility is negated.

This calls for quick sidestepping and the use of techniques which force him into poor choices. Each choice must place you at an advantage. In short you must manoeuvre in order to ambush him.

Once you have outmanoeuvred him, the maximum effort must be expended in punishing his body, thereby robbing him of the stamina necessary to continually move.

Timing, distance and mobility are areas that demand much study and experimentation. An appreciation of your own strengths and weaknesses will assist in making progress. Remember that consistency, like hesitancy, works against timing. Your continual aim should be to deceive and wrong-foot your opponent.

Distance is individual, varying according to your opponent's and your own abilities. Distance fluctuates throughout a fight and is affected by the dominant fighter and his own preferences.

The method by which timing, distance and mobility are sharpened is sparring.

Chapter Six: Sparring

Sparring is the method by which skills are blended and sharpened. It is the greatest indicator of a fighter's preparedness for the ring.

Yet sparring is not fighting, and here we have a paradox; it is the nearest thing to fighting, yet ultimately is nothing like it.

To understand this paradox we have to look at what happens in sparring when a fighter is stunned. In the gym the coach will step in and allow the dazed man to recover in order that the learning process can continue, yet in the ring the very second a fighter is stunned, his opponent will launch a ferocious all-out attack. The psychology of the two are a million miles apart.

Sparring is a training method and a means by which the coach or trainer assesses the kick boxer, it possesses the flavour, but not the essence, of real fighting.

At the end of the Introduction I quoted my instructor Geoff Britton as saying 'the gym is your laboratory.' An obvious interpretation of this is that the gym is a place for experimentation, but I always believed it to go beyond simply that; by implication it also says 'the gym is not an arena'.

Sparring should always be conducted safely, without fear and with an open and questioning attitude.

Reckless sparring helps no one. Your gym partners are not the enemy. On the other hand, as skills and conditioning increase so should the pace and power of sparring. The coach should be present at all times to control, advise and encourage.

For many, sparring at a kick boxing club will be the final goal. The sheer enjoyment and exhilaration of this contact sport is a perfectly reasonable end in itself, however, many will want to go on to fight in the ring, therefore this chapter will address both aims.

Safety Equipment

Before undertaking sparring, a fighter must obtain for him or herself the necessary safety equipment. These items are not optional extras, but are vital to safe sparring.

1) Head Guard

This should be of the 'open-face' type. Head guards with cheek pieces blind you to kicks that come from the floor.

2) Groin Guard

This should be the full boxing-type groin guard which also protects the lower abdomen. The absolute minimum you should wear is a martial arts box-type guard.

3) Breast Guard

For female fighters breast guards are essential. The hard moulded plastic variety offers the best protection.

4) Gumshield

A gumshield should be well fitting and stay in position at all times. The 'hot water' self-moulding type is acceptable providing you take the trouble to mould it correctly. The best option is one made by a dental technician.

5) Gloves

In general fighters over 64 kg should spar with 16 oz gloves, and those below 64 kg with 14 oz ones. As the date of the fight grows nearer, the coach may opt to reduce the weight of the gloves to provide more realistic impact. However, these should not be below 10 oz for fighters above 64 kg and 8oz for fighters below that.

6) Shin/Instep Protectors

Foam boot-type instep protection should be worn in conjunction with shin protectors. As with all protective equipment, these should be snug fitting and secure.

6) Hand-Wraps

Hand-wraps should be worn during sparring, heavy bag and focus pad work. The bones of the hands are small and easily damaged. The hand-wraps bind these in such a way as to protect the knuckles, base of the thumb and the wrist. The correct way to bandage your hands is shown in diagrams 14 to 18.

In figs. 189 and 190, both male and female fighters are shown properly equipped to undertake sparring.

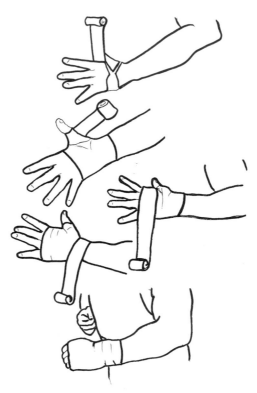

Diagrams 14, 15, 16, 17 and 18

Fig. 189   *Fig. 190*

General Sparring

This is a form of 'free practice'. In this training method you use all your hand and leg techniques, both singularly and in combination whilst using timing, distance and mobility to achieve your ends.

This is what you have been training for, your entire repertoire of skills are finally being tested by a breathing, thinking opponent.

From day one of sparring you should keep a training diary into which all your areas of success and failure are entered. Make notes on everything that your coach and training partners tell you. Then add your own comments. Analysis is essential for a serious kick boxer.

Relative to this is the skill level of your opponent. Someone with the same background and period of training should have approximately the same degree of success, however with more or less experienced fighters, variations will obviously occur.

Height and weight will also be big factors, therefore, only by sparring with a large number of opponents will you be in a position to assess your own progress.

It has already been stated that there is a huge difference between sparring in the gym and fighting in the ring. Simply put, gym sparring is part of your training, part of the process that aims to improve your ability. Ring fighting has but one aim, victory.

Gym Sparring

Type 1: Opponent of Equal Ability

Generally, when sparring with an opponent of equal ability you should use only your sharpest techniques. When physical ability and experience are equal, the man that wins is the man who out-thinks his opponent. Tactics are the key.

Type 2: Opponent of Inferior Ability

When sparring against an opponent of inferior ability you should not switch off just because you have the advantage. Use the opportunity to apply new ideas and techniques.

Occasionally you should limit yourself to a few selected techniques so as to sharpen their timing and variation. Used correctly, sparring with an opponent of inferior ability can be one of the most productive and worthwhile sessions.

Type 3: Opponent of Superior Ability

It is in this situation that you will feel the most pressure. Against the superior opponent you should use everything you have got.

Start by noting what type of fighter he is, aggressive, counter-puncher, hit and run raider etc, then try to bring the fight on to your terms. The aim when fighting the superior opponent is to bring your strongest weapons against his weakest defences, therefore 'test' him and learn quickly.

Gym sparring is about the refinement of skills. Your whole approach should be governed by observation, experimentation, self-analysis and personal improvement.

Ring Fighting

In the ring there is one victor. Your aim when stepping in the ring is to bring your skills to bear against an opponent of approximately equal ability and weight. In order for you to be successful, you must observe your opponent and then use that knowledge to bring about his defeat as quickly as possible.

To do this you must apply tactics that force your opponent to fight the way that suits you.

Tactics

1) Lure or pressure your opponent into your best or chosen technique.

2) Set him problems, then punish him when he attempts to remedy them, for example retreat to create more distance, then jam him as he moves in.

3) Dominate him by:

   a) Hitting hard.

   b) Hitting with maximum speed.

   c) Keeping him reacting to your tactics rather than initiating his own.

4) Use variety in attack and defence to stop his attempts at reading you.

5) Observe any patterns in his approach, then choose the tactics to foil them.

6) The name of the game is deception – think of disguising the way you use techniques and combinations.

Tactics against Specific Types of Opponent

The opening rounds of a fight should be spent in reconnaissance so that you can use effective techniques against your opponent. Sometimes he will fall broadly into a particular category and because these types will recur in your ring career, you must have some flexible tactics to deal with them.

Opponent of Superior Reach

An opponent of superior reach must be countered by side-to-side head movements to make him miss with his lead punches. Defensive combinations should also be used to punish his attempts at keeping you at distance.

If you are stronger, then get inside and stay there, making him work at a disadvantage. As with any and all advantages enjoyed by your opponent, you must improvise solutions based on your own strengths.

If your opponent has a longer reach and is a kicking specialist, deflect his straight line kicks, such as front kicks and side kicks, with lower parries and counter with strong crosses followed up by other punches. When inside stay there.

Against his circular techniques, such as roundhouse kicks and hook kicks, take the kick on a right or left arm cover, and then move inside. A kicker should always be denied room to work.

The Southpaw Opponent

A southpaw opponent with good timing is the hardest man to fight (Fig. 191). There is an old saying, 'Southpaws should be strangled at birth!' The reasons why southpaws are so difficult to deal with are many.

Fig. 191

To begin with the timing on your lead hand will be thrown out. Secondly all your favourite combinations will require adjustment. Thirdly attacks will come at you from different angles and lastly, the hesitation that these problems cause are the perfect opportunity for your southpaw opponent to attack.

The orthodox wisdom for fighting southpaws is to throw strong right hand punches and kicks. However, you must remember that a southpaw fights orthodox opponents virtually the whole time and will be more than wise to both your problems and the standard methods for dealing with them.

The tendency for an orthodox fighter confronting a southpaw is to use lead hand parries. This should be avoided at all times.

It sets you up for a strong overhand cross and will place you at a severe disadvantage by tying up your own lead hand, which is one of the main distance gaugers.

Southpaws - Three strategies and a Fourth Option

Strategy 1: Fight out of a natural guard, but attack with multiple combinations to force him on to the back foot. Open with fast jabs and lead kicks, use lead sweeps to disturb and agitate him, then timed rear punches and kicks to exploit the openings. Do not let him lead, keep him reacting rather than initiating.

Strategy 2: Fight out of a natural guard, but use timed crosses and rear leg kicks as openers (do not throw them 'cold') then flow into a suitable combination, in effect making the first technique of your favoured combination the second of your 'southpaw' adaptation. e.g. timed cross followed by an orthodox jab/cross/roundhouse.

Strategy 3: Fight out of a southpaw stance yourself. This requires considerable previous training and should not be attempted without it.

Strategy 4: Fight using all three previous strategies, changing constantly to agitate and confuse him.

Aggressive Heavy Puncher

This type of opponent will hunt you around the ring. He will advance by smothering your kicks and punishing you hard to the body and head. He is confident in his power and his one aim is to let you feel it.

His confidence is his strength and also his Achilles heel. You must destroy his confidence with a combination of sweeps and counters.

In order for him to unload he must have a solid base and by sweeping away his base you stop him from hitting you. Work from behind a tight guard and never forget that you must not take your hands away from what they are trying to protect.

Also use straight kicks such as front kicks and side kicks as stop-hits.

Structured Sparring

During your training you will from time to time experience problems that frustrate you and prevent progression, such as an inability to use the jab correctly or failure to deal with close-in fighting. To overcome these problems you will have to resort to structured sparring. This is sparring under special conditions with the specific aim of forcing you to work on your weaknesses.

We have already seen and read in Chapter Three, two 'structured methods' of sparring, on the wall and tied sparring. These two methods test and hone defensive skills, however, many other forms exist.

Hands Only

This is an excellent method of starting a sparring session because it tightens up your guard. In a typical sparring session you may want to do six or seven rounds; make the first three hands only and then combine hands and legs for the remainder.

Jab versus Jab

This is used mainly with novice kick boxers who fail to lead correctly and lunge in without timing or reason. The first two rounds of a sparring session should be jab versus jab until a marked improvement is shown in a kick boxer's ability to use a 'timed' lead.

Hands versus Hands and Legs

Many fighters stay at range and pick at their opponents. There is nothing wrong with this, but in a novice kick boxer it is frequently a sign of nervousness and hesitation. By making him fight with hands against hands and legs he will have to break down the gap and move inside.

Close Sparring

Fifty per cent of fighting is done at close range. As a rule of thumb, the more success your opponent has, the closer he wants to get.

Close sparring is performed by standing toe-to-toe with your opponent and sparring with both hands and legs (Fig. 192). This is a very tiring way of fighting and at first you will want to move away and buy yourself some room.

Fig. 192

Experiment with full guard, half guard and cross guard. Look to hit around the edges of your opponent's guard and when he spreads his elbows to cover this, switch to uppercuts and lead leg front kicks through the middle. When he brings his arms together to cover this, switch back to hooks around the edges. Take the initiative and keep it.

Try to fight from behind a tight defence by always having 'one hand back at base' i.e. one hand guarding whilst the other works.

Lean into your opponent, resting your lead shoulder on him. This makes him expend energy by pushing back. The secret is not to push, but to use your weight - you rest whilst he works.

Frustrate his attempts at using a short cross by raising your lead shoulder. Frustrate his attempts at uppercutting by leaning on the blow with your lead forearm.

Control his left arm by pressing on his left elbow.

If you hold his elbow continually the referee will intervene, the secret is to use your hand as a 'sensor' so that just as he tries to hit with that arm you press against it then release before the referee can object.

Remember, holding is not allowed, but pressing is borderline and providing it is not overused, is a good tool.

Power when working close comes from forceful twisting of the hips and correct body alignment, not from large limb actions which can be seen and avoided.

A particularly effective technique is the short cross combined with a lead shoulder withdrawal. First you pull back your lead shoulder barely enough to accommodate your glove. Then snap a short cross at an angle between your shoulder and his body. Lastly, withdraw your glove and reposition your lead shoulder so as to close the gap. (Figs. 193 and 194)

Fig. 193

Fig. 194

Shovel hooks and orthodox hooks combined with uppercuts are the bread and butter tools when close, whilst the judicious use of lead leg front kicks and sweeps will agitate and weaken your opponent.

It is suggested that you work at close sparring until you feel completely comfortable with it. In the ring you will have no choice.

Tag Sparring

This is a club practice method and a good tool for the coach when deciding whether a fighter is ready for the ring. Its aim is to give you practice at shorts burst of sustained pressure. The kind of pressure that most fighters wilt under in their first few contests.

Practice Method

Take a group of ten individuals of various abilities and split them into two groups of five. Now pick out one fighter from each group and let them commence sparring. The idea is for each group to stay ahead by substituting (tagging) their fighter before he runs out of steam. Equally they can 'tag' their fighter immediately after he has landed a series of good shots, thereby keeping the initiative. (Fig. 195)

Fig. 195

The coach can assume responsibility for tagging so as to keep the sparring intense and free-flowing. Safety is also a factor and care must be taken when matching fighters of widely differing weights and abilities.

Waiting fighters should be encouraged to call out advice, thereby sharpening their own observation and analytical skills.

This type of training brings out a positive club spirit and marries two normally opposite mental attitudes – fun and pressure.

Analysis of Sparring

It was mentioned at the beginning of this chapter that you should keep a training diary so as to record and analyse your workouts and it cannot be stressed enough how valuable this is, however, there are other ways in which you can learn more about your own abilities. Perhaps the most useful of these is video recording sparring.

Frequently when you are corrected by the coach it is difficult to understand or accept criticisms made. By watching the incident or incidents on a television screen you will be able to appreciate them far more easily.

The use of slow motion, freeze frame and normal playback can isolate the problem and assist the coach in helping you eradicate it.

When the problem has been identified then focus pad work, structured sparring and pair work can eliminate it.

Naturally when your actual fights in the ring have been recorded, you should obtain a copy and study it. Write down everything you see.

The modern kick boxer must learn to be self-critical and to use all the aids that are available to help him progress. Pride must never be allowed to obstruct progress.

Guidelines For Fighting In The Ring

1) Always think, even when tired or scared.

2) Use combinations, not single blows.

3) Fight at your pace, not his or hers.

4) Do not repeat mistakes – that's the way to get beaten.

5) Never give up. Strive to overcome your opponent using all your skills.

6) Remember, you work against yourself by . . .

   a) Failing to use your knowledge.

   b) Being unfit.

   c) Mentally conceding.

   d) Ceasing to strive for greater ability.

Frequency of Sparring

For reasons of safety and to maintenance of peak fitness, sparring should be carried out on alternate days only, e.g. Monday/Wednesday/Friday.

The days in between can be used for pad and bag work and all other aspects of training.

A recommended schedule for the training week is given in Chapter Nine.

Summary

Several times in this chapter mention has been made of the necessity for an analytical approach to training. It is only by 'switching-on' that a fighter can achieve **maximum skill up-take**.

Below is a short list that emphasises the methods and practices that assist this process.

1) Informed observation of yourself and others.

2) Note Taking: Keep a training diary and write down everything that you, your coach and training partners notice, that way you will not have to constantly rediscover your errors.

3) Video recording your training and actual fights in the ring is a priceless aid to observation. Use freeze frame, slow motion and normal speed playback and compare what you see to your training diary notes.

4) Use structured sparring to isolate and work particular skills and solve problems. Use the suggested methods and do not be afraid to devise others.

5) Remember above all that being self-critical is not being negative, but is the root of progress.

Chapter Seven: Speed And Power

With the basic skills learnt, distance, timing and mobility concepts absorbed and sparring established as the determining test of your ability, we can now turn our attention to two important areas which reinforce our skills: speed and power.

Speed of hitting alone can sting, confuse and ultimately defeat your opponent. It has many uses in both attack and defence and is acquired initially by pure repetition, but in order to reach your maximum potential speed, you must isolate its constituent parts and exercise them. Only when all extraneous movement and thought is shed can you obtain true speed.

The Structure of Speed

There are three elements that make up speed:

1) Limb Speed: fast hands and legs that deliver the attack or defence once in position.

2) Body Speed: fast footwork that carries the body into position the instant a stimulus is received.

3) Reflex Speed: reaction to a stimulus that delivers the correct skill in response to an attack – counter, defence or attack on the presentation of an opportunity.

Limb Speed

Another word for this is technique. Having been taught a particular skill the kick boxer must spend many hours repeating the movements so that the action flows easily and all unnecessary motion is shed.

The body must be relaxed before exploding into action – tension works against you.

Throwing a technique over and over again has long been recognised in the eastern martial arts as a way of self-instruction. Do a thousand repetitions and let your body learn the necessary co-ordination. Do another thousand and achieve snap. Do another thousand and throw more body weight into the technique. Do another thousand until the action is explosive. Do another thousand and . . . you get the picture.

Pure repetition will give you limb speed. Do not underestimate the body's ability to learn. Your brain is happiest with both repetition and patterns of movement, once it has learnt what is expected, it will release the body and the technique will fly.

To maintain speed requires constant practice, to improve speed requires greater effort still.

'Another thousand' is no mean slogan for the aspiring kick boxer.

Fig. 196

Body Speed

Unless a fighter can quickly close the gap between himself and the opponent, limb speed is useless.

The very second that you initiate your movement you will be seen. If you are slow, you will never arrive at the place you need to be in order to let your techniques go.

During this movement phase your opponent will either move away, or counter. The longer you take, the more time he has to prepare a warm reception for you.

Mobility has been covered in some depth in Chapter Five. Here we are concerned only with fast footwork that transports the body into or out of range at top speed.

Time must be given over in the gym to practising footwork alone. Clumsy or heavy footwork must be replaced with a lightness of movement. Always ensure that the rear heel is up and the knees are bent in readiness to straighten the leg.

Once you detect an attack or an opportunity to deliver one of your own, you must let the body fly. Practise this by taking up a position at natural fighting range from a bag. Mark the distance with a chalk line (Fig. 196). At a given signal, drive in rapidly and let your combination go. Have somebody watch, or better still video, your efforts at closing the gap.

Reflex Speed

Quickness of the eye is of utmost importance to a kick boxer. The sooner he sees an opportunity or a threat, the more time he will have to prepare a correct response.

Limb speed and body speed are made redundant if the correct moment to respond is missed.

In the summary at the end of Chapter One it was said that 'it takes 5,000 repetitions to make a physical action an instantaneous reflex.'

The brain needs time to learn what is expected and the body needs to practise the actions so that the muscles are completely relaxed. However, 'quickness of the eye' is what impels your physical response and it is this area of speed that must be exercised the most.

The focus pads are without doubt the best tool for developing reflex speed.

Have a partner hold two focus pads close to his chest. Take up a position at a natural fighting range and again mark it with chalk. Your partner should snap up the pads and call a combination. Your reflex is measured by the time it takes you to start moving and the total speed of your attack is measured from the point of stimulus, i.e. when the pads snap up, until you have finished the combination.

Once again the video camera is a superb aid to monitor your progress. Slow motion and freeze frame playback will show the 'time lag' between the pads snapping up and your initial movement.

Vary the distance at which you work - long range, middle range and close range. Obviously the nearer you are, the greater the emphasis on reflex speed and the less on body speed and limb speed.

Kicks should be worked exactly the same as hands. Your training partner should snap up the focus pads and simultaneously call out a kick or a punch/kick combination.

The most basic combinations can be numbered, for example jab/cross = 1, jab/cross/hook = 2, jab/roundhouse to body = 3 etc, and instead of calling techniques, the focus pad holder can simply call out a number. Some fight camps take this practice further and call numbered combinations to fighters in the ring.

Speed Summary

1) Keep the body relaxed, especially the attacking limb.

2) Footwork must be explosive – slow fighters get ambushed.

3) Reflex Speed is essential in order to seize opportunities.

Speed is related to power. The faster you move the greater the potential impact.

Power

Power is the technical application of force to the target.

Strength is only the body's potential to apply force. Power is the actual amount of bodily strength delivered to the opponent's target area. It has to be realised that a strong man is not necessarily a strong puncher or kicker.

This is not to dismiss strength, merely to set it in context. Its importance is fully outlined in Chapter Eight.

Technique and power are of equal importance to the kick boxer. An overreliance on one or the other is dangerous. Therefore the kick boxer must spend considerable time on the big bag so that both technique and power are developed together.

As with speed, the body must be relaxed so that limbs fly.

Techniques may be trained separately at first, but ultimately you must train with combinations.

Practice Method One: The Big Bag

Select a technique or combination and take up position before the big bag. Throw ten repetitions of the technique as hard as you can. Shake your arms free and throw another ten, shake your arms free again and throw a third set of ten. Now move on to the next chosen technique or combination.

The aim should always be to hit explosively and this means accelerating throughout the technique and sinking the blows deep into the middle of the big bag.

Power is obtained by multiplying mass by speed or to put it another way, by putting as much of your body weight as possible behind a technique that is travelling at top speed.

Thirty full power repetitions of each of your selected techniques and combinations is a good base, but the aim must always be for more power and more speed. Hold nothing back. The bag will 'jump' if you hit it correctly but will merely swing away if you push it.

You must 'time' the bag. For straight punches and kicks swing the bag away from you and the instant it starts to swing back, hit it. (Fig. 197)

For round and circular punches and kicks swing the bag from side to side. Again you hit it just as it starts to swing back to the centre. (Fig. 198)

Fig. 197   *Fig. 198*

You must accelerate throughout the technique.

Only by spending many hours on the big bag will your potential be reached. A minimum of two sessions a week should be given over to the big bag. Three is better, working on the principle of alternate day work-outs. Power training should follow on from sparring.

As we have already stated, power is force delivered to the target; if the target is mobile then you must logically practise delivering power on the move. For this we must go back to the focus pads.

Practice Method Two: Focus Pads

Both the kick boxer and the focus pad holder must move around as though fighting. The pad holder calls a combination and the kick boxer drives in with everything he has. Incorporate upper body movement such as slipping, ducking, bobbing and weaving for maximum realism.

Correct body alignment is essential and the pad holder must constantly correct the kick boxer: rotation of heels, hips and shoulders in hooks and uppercuts; head, shoulder and hip turn in spinning backfist, spinning backthrust and spinning hook kicks; rear leg movement in crosses; hip drive, foot rotation and knee snap in roundhouse kicks and so on. (Fig. 199)

Fig. 199

The greater the distance from the target, the more speed can be generated and therefore the more power possible. Close in, power comes more from explosive twists and rotations of the body.

With correct body mechanics, knockout power can be generated without large limb movements. Experiment with hooks and uppercuts to gain the feel of this.

When developing mobile power in thrust or spinning kicks, the kick shield is superior to focus pads.

Practice Method Three: Kick Shield

This is a good point to remind you that the five most effective kicks are all to the body. A power kick driven into the stomach can end a fight.

As with the focus pads the holder must move around as through fighting and call out certain kicks. (Fig. 200)

Fig. 200

Never aim at the surface of the shield, but drive through it. There are many types of power obtainable with kicks - thrust, snap, spin and whip. Some, such as snap and whip are hard to assess on a shield, so these must be worked on the focus pads.

There can be a tendency for kick boxers to throw lazy, sluggish kicks when tired and to rely on body weight alone to impart power. This should be vigorously discouraged. A slow kick will be countered heavily.

Power Summary

Three key factors for Power:
1) Keep the body relaxed.
2) Put as much body weight as fast as you can behind each technique.
3) Accelerate throughout the technique.

Chapter Eight: Conditioning

The building of a strong and agile body is the physical foundation for success. When all other factors are equal, the strongest fighter will win.

Conditioning is vital for a kick boxer for he will have to endure as well as administer hard blows.

The other side of the coin is that all too frequently stamina and strength are resorted to in place of skill. This may bring one or two early victories for the novice kick boxer, but ultimately it is a dead-end.

When you step into the ring, whether it is for three, five, seven, nine or twelve rounds, you must be fit in order that your skills can be used to their maximum potential. To this end it must always be borne in mind that you lose energy in three distinct ways:

1) By throwing your own techniques.
2) By absorption of energy-sapping blows.
3) By nervous tension which affects your normal breathing pattern.

The temptation for a kick boxer to take a fight when unfit must be resisted. It is not fair to himself and is potentially dangerous. Injuries occur most when fatigue has set in. The Red Army used the motto 'Train hard fight easy' – it captures the essence of this chapter.

Four areas must be covered for you to be completely conditioned for the ring.
1) Flexibility
2) Stamina
3) Strength
4) Co-ordination

Flexibility

Flexibility is the range of joint movement and muscle elasticity. Without it the kick boxer will not obtain the maximum muscle efficiency or achieve height with kicks. Quite simply, your body will be competing against itself.

Many kick boxers come from other martial arts backgrounds and will be familiar with stretching exercises, so for them what follows may not be new, but that does not in any way diminish its importance.

Flexibility exercises should be performed daily, before and after training.

Before commencing flexibility exercises you must warm your body thoroughly. Running on the spot or skipping for three or four rounds will bring up the body temperature thus causing the blood vessels to expand and pump warming blood through the muscles. Never stretch when cold.

Joint Manipulation

1) **The Neck**
Rotate the head gently clockwise (Diagram 19). Then anticlockwise. Next, turn your head to the left (Diagram 20), then to the right. Next tip the head back (Diagram 21) then forward. (Diagram 22)

2) **The Shoulders**
Stand normally. Swing your arm forward in a circle (Diagram 23). Next, swing it backwards. Repeat with the other arm.

3) **The Waist**
Stand with your feet one shoulder width apart. Place your hands on your hips. Now rotate your hips in a circle, first one way and then the other. (Diagram 24)

4) **The Hips**
Lift your right leg until your thigh is parallel to the ground. Now rotate your hip in a circle. Repeat with the left leg. (Diagram 25)

5) **The Knees**
Stand with your feet together and place your hands on your knees. Bend your knees and rotate your legs first to the left and then to the right. (Diagram 26)

6) **The Ankles**
Lift your right leg until your thigh is parallel with the ground. Rotate your right foot in a circle. Now repeat with the left foot. (Diagram 27)

Diagrams 19, 20, 21 and 22

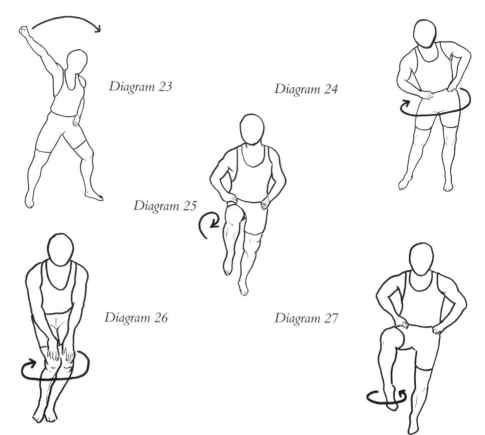

Diagram 23

Diagram 24

Diagram 25

Diagram 26

Diagram 27

Stretching

There are two types of stretching: **static** and **ballistic**.

Static stretching is when the stretch is held in position, whereas ballistic stretching is when the muscles being stretched are moved through an arc - rather similar to kicking with the knee locked straight.

Ballistic stretching should follow static stretching so as to prevent injury.

You must never 'bounce' during a stretch, because you can 'bounce' past the point of injury and tear muscles.

Box Splits

Box splits stretch the inside of the thighs (Diagram 28). Spread your legs as far as you can and hold the stretch for one minute. You should feel some discomfort, but not pain. If you experience pain shorten the stretch.

Now press down with the soles of your feet into the floor for ten seconds. Release and extend your stretch another few inches. Hold for a further minute.

Splits

Splits stretch the underneath of your thigh (Diagram 29). Spread your legs apart with the left leg in front. The knee of your lead leg should be straight. Bend the rear leg as much as is necessary. The heel of your lead leg should be on the floor with your hands either side of the lead leg to maintain balance. Hold for one minute. Now press down with your lead heel into the floor for ten seconds. Release and extend the stretch. Hold for a further minute. Now turn 180 degrees and repeat with the right leg in front.

It is usual to first perform the box splits and then the normal splits. You should repeat the exercises going from one to the other three or four times.

Diagram 28

Diagram 29

Diagrams 30, 31 and 32

Lower Back Stretch

This, as the name suggests, stretches the lower back and is a particularly important stretch for the kick boxer.

Spread your legs in a box splits. Now sit down leaving your legs apart (Diagram 30). Stretch your body along your right leg, grasp your foot or ankle and try to get your head down on to the knee (Diagram 31). Hold for ten seconds. Repeat with the left leg.

Repeat several times increasing the length of the hold time by ten seconds each time.

Now hold both feet and try to get your head down on to the floor (Diagram 32). Hold the stretch for ten seconds. Repeat several times increasing the holding time by ten seconds each time.

Full Back Stretch

This exercise fully extends the back and is particularly useful when your back has tightened up after a previous training session.

Lie on the floor and drag your heels hard along the floor until you reach your bottom (Diagram 33). Now draw up your legs to your chest and wrap your arms around your knees (Diagram 34). Hold for ten seconds. Release, then push your heels into the ground until your legs are fully extended (Diagram 35). Repeat several times.

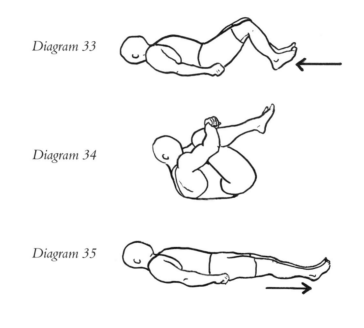

Diagram 33

Diagram 34

Diagram 35

Groin Stretch

This stretches the inside of the groin area, a region particularly affected by strenuous kicks.

Sit down and draw up your feet to your groin, placing the soles of your feet together (Diagram 36). Now press down with your elbows on your knees. Hold for ten seconds and again repeat several times.

Standing Groin Stretch

This exercise is well known in martial arts circles and is commonly called horse stance.

Stand with your legs three feet apart. Now perform a semi-squat until your thighs are parallel to the ground (Diagram 37). Hold for one minute. Release and shake your legs free. Now assume the semi-squat position again for one minute. Repeat several times.

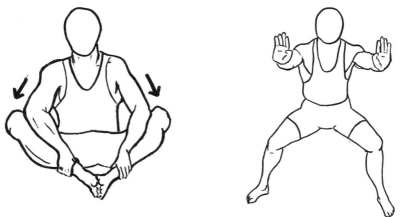

Diagram 36   *Diagram 37*

Ballistic Stretching

Straight Swing

Stand with one foot in front of the other about three feet apart (Diagram 38). Now, keeping your leg straight throughout, swing you rear foot forward and upward as far as possible (Diagram 39). Repeat ten times with each leg.

Diagrams 38 and 39

Circular Swing

This is very similar to the martial arts technique known as the crescent kick.

Stand as in the straight swing, again keeping your leg straight, swing your leg across your body and then out so that the leg swings through an arc (Diagram 40). Repeat ten times with each leg.

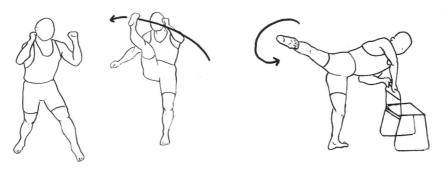

Diagram 40   *Diagram 41*

Back Swing

Hold on to a chair. Now raise your right leg keeping it straight. Swing the leg slowly in a circle towards your rear (Diagram 41). Repeat ten times with each leg.

Summary

1) Always warm the body before commencing flexibility exercises.
2) Manipulate the joints prior to stretching.
3) Never 'bounce' whilst stretching.

Stamina

Stamina, also known as endurance and cardio-vascular fitness, is vital to the kick boxer. In order to use your fighting skills to the maximum you must have the capacity to keep going throughout the entire fight.

Windows of opportunity, either created by you or through an error on the part of your opponent, must be capitalised on quickly. If you need to gulp air before moving, the opportunity will be lost.

There are no short cuts to stamina. The foundations for a successful fighting career have to be laid down over months and years. Naturally if you aim for the very top then your foundations must go deep. It is also well to remember that breaks in your fighting year, brought about by injury or illness, will affect your stamina. A break of one month may take two months of 'rehabilitation' to put you back on track.

There are four main methods for attaining and maintaining stamina:
1) Running
2) Skipping
3) Cycling
4) Swimming

For the purposes of kick boxing we need only consider the first two methods.

Running

Putting in the Base

The foundation or base for stamina comes from L.S.D. – Long Slow Distance running (jogging). The most important thing is to start with a relatively easy regime, say two miles every other day (alternating with skills sessions in the gym) and then build up gradually to five miles over a period of six months.

This may seem modest, but it should be remembered that the idea is to become a good kick boxer not a runner and overtraining is worse than undertraining. It is also true that if you push too hard too soon you will sustain injuries.

You will find that as you get fitter your times for the runs will get shorter. However, a number of months into this routine improvements in your running times will diminish or stop. You have hit the first of many plateaus and this is the signal that the time is getting near to change your running routine.

The base should be 200 miles of L.S.D. which is comfortably achievable over six months. At this point it is necessary to change the type of runs to (a) improve your speed and (b) more closely resemble the rhythm and pace of kick boxing. So having achieved the base we are ready for *fartlek*.

Fartlek

The term *fartlek* comes from a Swedish word meaning 'speedplay'. Another term for this is varied pace running. The idea is to vary the demands on your oxygen needs, sometimes taking you into the realms of anaerobic running (without oxygen) where your body works so fast that you cannot process the oxygen you need fast enough.

So, instead of running say three or four miles steadily, you vary the pace: ½ mile of L.S.D. to thoroughly warm and prepare the body then 100 metres walk/100 metres jog/100 metres run/100 metres sprint/ and back to 100 metres walk/100 jog etc for a mile and a half and then back to L.S.D. for a final half-mile warm down.

As a car uses up petrol faster around the town than when driving on a motorway, your body will use up energy much faster. Your first few sessions of *fartlek* will 'hurt'.

If you think about the way you fight, you will realise it is in bursts of action similar to *fartlek*. This makes this type of running extremely useful for a kick boxer.

The by-product of this is that the sprint phases of *fartlek* force your body to work harder than normal and this will increase your ability to speed up when required.

We have already said that you should be running on alternate days, three to four times a week - now make just one of those sessions a *fartlek* run.

A typical week's running schedule for a six-month kick boxer should look something like this:

Monday: 5 miles L.S.D.
Wednesday: 2½ miles *fartlek*: ½ mile warm-up - 1½ miles *fartlek*
             - ½ mile warm down.
Friday: 3 mile medium/fast pace run.

The example given for *fartlek* is a basic one.
You can of course vary not only the pace, but also the distances,
e.g. 100 metre walk/50 metre jog/50 metre run/25 metre sprint.

Fartlek was created originally to take some of the grind and boredom out of running for athletes, but it might have been created for kick boxers, so perfectly does it fulfil our needs.

Hill/Steps Running

There is much misinformation about what you should and should not do in terms of improving your stamina. You may have heard of kick boxers who swear by running up and down steps and also using hills as a means to increasing the difficulty factor of running. Both of these methods have benefits, however it is strongly recommended that hill and steps work-outs are done in off-season periods such as during a Christmas or midsummer break.

The reason for this is that both these methods serve to increase your leg strength and base, but the price for this is a drop in speed. Remember each phase of running serves a different purpose and to do hill or steps work-outs leading up to a fight is counter-productive.

Interval Running

If you have put in the base and then followed the above or a similar routine for an additional six months, you will now be ready for interval work.

The concept of interval work is to break up your run into a series of explosive bursts interspersed with jog recovery intervals. Using this method it is possible to make your body work harder than running the same distance at a fast rate.

Do not take short cuts – only attempt interval sessions after preparing correctly.

The Interval Session

1) Run L.S.D. for one mile.
2) Jog for one minute.
3) Run 4 x 400 metre sprints with a minute's slow jog recovery in between each 400 metres.
4) Jog for one minute.
5) Run 2 x 200 metre sprints with a minute's slow jog recovery in between.
6) Jog for one minute.
7) Run 2 x 100 metre sprints with a minute's slow jog recovery in between.
8) Run ½ mile L.S.D. as a warm-down.
The distances can be adjusted, however, this is very hard training and the recovery intervals should be of at least one minute's duration.

Summary

Running should be thought of as a pyramid. L.S.D. forms the base. *Fartlek* the middle and interval sessions the top. (Diagram 42)

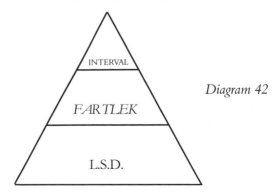

Diagram 42

L.S.D. will lower your pulse rate and improve your oxygen uptake (aerobic running).

Fartlek will give you speed and introduce your body to anaerobic (without oxygen) running.

Interval sessions will give you explosive acceleration and enhanced anaerobic capability - the icing on the cake.

Skipping

Skipping can be used in place of running providing that the same principles are incorporated.

Some kick boxers prefer skipping because it can be performed indoors during inclement weather. Further, the exact rhythm and pace of a fight can be applied – bursts of action can be interspersed with steady, fast and sprint skipping.

The types of step may also be varied. For steady state work merely bounce from one foot to the other. As the pace increases, start to lift your knees up until your thighs are parallel with the floor. Double skips where you pass the rope around twice without your feet touching the floor and walking skips where you jump the legs forwards and backwards on each rope pass - like walking - may also be used. Lastly you can literally run as you skip – both forwards and backwards.

Putting in the Base

Skip for fifteen minutes every other day. Build to thirty minutes per session over a period of six months.

As an alternative you can skip for rounds. i.e ten rounds of three minutes duration interspersed with one-minute recovery periods. This, it should be emphasised, is steady state skipping.

Fartlek Skipping

Skip steadily for ten minutes to warm up. Now go 'on the clock' and skip for eight rounds with bursts of five, ten and twenty seconds flat out skipping linked with steady state skipping as recovery. Do not sprint again until you have control of your breathing. Warm down with five minutes of steady state skipping.

Fartlek skipping approximates fighting more closely than any other form of exercise due to the degree of control that you have on the speed of the rope.

Which ever you choose, running or skipping, you must resist the urge to merely 'churn out the miles'. If your stamina training is to be of use to you, then it must reflect as accurately as possible the variable tempo of a fight.

Finally, if further proof is needed, when Michael Spinks became the only Light Heavy Weight in the history of professional boxing to win the World Heavy Weight Title it was largely because of his trainer, who came from an athletics background. He immediately stopped Spinks from running ten miles every day - his reasoning was that Spinks had his base, why continue? Next he asked a simple and very telling question, 'What are you training for?' The answer was, 'For twelve rounds of boxing.'

So, Spinks needed to fight for three minutes with a minutes recovery in between – interval sessions – from that moment on he was put on a regime of interval sessions that enabled him to work flat out for three minutes and to recover totally between rounds. His success was a vindication of the training changes, yet professional boxing has been slow to acknowledge it.

This is of course a long way from merely jogging two miles every other day, but there are no short cuts. Slow and measured increases of distance, speed and duration are the keys to improvement. The way to achieve this is to record your training, so that you can keep control. It should now be apparent why the use of a training diary is of such benefit to the kick boxer.

In the next chapter there are suggested schedules, mileages and routines that will bring together many of the skills and conditioning recommendations into a balanced programme for both the novice, intermediate and experienced kick boxer.

We now move on to yet another area steeped in controversy. Strength, and again the question has to be posed, 'What are you training for?'

Strength

Weight and resistance training are rightfully acknowledged as good ways to build muscle, but what type of muscle and how much?

Muscles work by contraction – pulling. Contraction both straightens and bends the limbs which we need to execute fast and strong techniques, therefore explosive contraction is the aim, not size, not shape and never cosmetics.

Muscle also serves another function: armour. This is particularly so of the muscles in the abdominal region, a large and vulnerable target. An old and very wise saying in boxing circles is, 'Kill the body and the head dies!'

Arms

The muscles that straighten the arms are the triceps at the back of the upper arm. These are the muscles used when you throw straight arm techniques such as jabs and crosses.

The muscles that bend the arm are the biceps at the front of the upper arm. These are the muscles used when you throw curved techniques such as hooks and uppercuts.

Some techniques such as the spinning backfist require you to first bend your arm and pull it in close to your body and then as you spin, to straighten it. Many techniques require this dual tasking of the muscles.

Sets and Reps

In order to work out how many repetitions of each exercise you should be doing, you must see how many repetitions of the exercise you can achieve in one go. Then do two thirds of this figure for each set and three sets of each exercise.

Example: Press-ups
You manage to do 30 press-ups in one go, so two thirds of 30 is 20 press-ups, which you do three times with a minute's rest in between each set.
20 press ups x 3 = 60.

This is a basic formula and as you progress you may wish to increase both the sets and the reps. A word of warning is necessary here. A kick boxer is not a weightlifter or for that matter a runner. Conditioning sessions are meant to augment not supplant skills sessions.

Triceps Exercises

Press-ups: The basic press-up (Diagrams 43 and 44), is a good way to build triceps strength. Note however that the further apart your arms are, the more the exercise works the pecs (chest muscles). Normally you should have your hands a shoulders width apart, but for advanced training you can move your hands further together. The ultimate is the hands at the mid-point of the body.

Dips: The dip (Diagrams 45 and 46) is a total body weight exercise and as such is very hard. It is though a superb builder of the triceps and is even harder than the press-up.

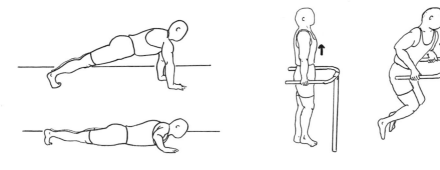

Diagrams 43 and 44   Diagrams 45 and 46

Many weight training exercises also build the triceps, such as the bench press and triceps extensions, however body weight exercises can be achieved without equipment and can therefore be performed anywhere.

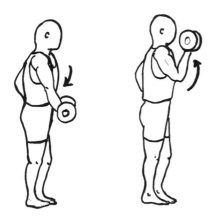

Biceps Exercises

Curls: Curls are performed using dumbells (Diagrams 47 and 48). Do not bend at the waist to assist the lifting action. Generally speaking, for kick boxing purposes it is better to use a light weight and many reps rather than heavy weights and a few reps.

Diagrams 47 and 48

Abdomen

A strong stomach and abdomen are essential. This region will come in for some heavy punishment during the course of a fight and once you are hurt in the body, your kicks will lose much of their power.

Both the upper and lower abdominal muscles must be firm and it is best if you pair up the exercises. e.g. Sit-ups followed by leg raises.

Sit-ups

Place your feet under a wall bar or something similar and draw your knees up so that your heels are near your bottom. Place your hands behind your head and point your elbows towards your knees (Diagram 49). Now sit up slowly and evenly and twist to touch your left knee with your right elbow (Diagram 50), and lower yourself back down. On the next rep turn so that your left elbow touches your right knee.

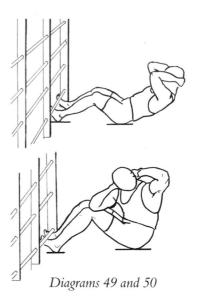

Diagrams 49 and 50

Leg Raises

Lie on your back with your legs straight and your toes pointed (Diagram 51), hold on to a wall bar or something similar and then slowly raise your legs until they are perpendicular to the floor (Diagram 52).

Diagrams 51 and 52

Concentric Crunches

Lie on your back with your hands behind your head and your legs out straight. Now simultaneously perform a Sit-up whilst bringing your knees up to touch your elbows (Diagram 53), exhale as you crunch and hold it for two to three seconds. This exercise will work both upper and lower abdominal muscles together.

Diagram 53

There are many forms of abdominal exercise and there is not space enough here to explore them in depth. It should be noted however that the abdominal muscles can be exercised daily whereas it is important to alternate days with all other weight and resistance exercises.

Legs

Quads and Hamstrings

It is recommended that you use hill running and steps works-outs to build the leg muscles. The type of strength required of a kick boxer's legs is best acquired by dynamic movement rather than through weight training.

Off season you can significantly increase the power of your legs by adjusting your running programme, aim to do two hill sessions per week.

Hill Session

Naturally the length and gradient of the hill must be taken into account, but a length of 100 metres should suffice. Treat it as you would an interval session. Run for a mile to warm up and then do a series of hill climbs with jogging back down as recovery. Ten climbs will test you. Then jog for a ½ mile as a warm-down.

Steps

The World Kick Boxing Champion Jean Yves Theriault used steps sessions to great effect and built some of the most effective kicks in the sport as a result.

The formula is the same as for hill sessions. Find a set of suitable steps and after a warm-up, run a series of steps before warming down over ½ a mile.

Hill and steps sessions will give you tremendous leg strength and put inches on your thighs. When this is added to technique, the effects can be devastating.

Co-ordination

Co-ordination is defined as the body's ability to carry out the brain's demands.

Many of the techniques of kick boxing require several actions to be performed simultaneously. For the novice this presents problems. What happens invariably is that the brain 'simplifies' the task because it cannot pick up all the subtleties at once.

Further, this problem is also encountered by the more experienced kick boxer learning a new skill for the first time, although generally, because of their other, related skills, they will pick up a new skill quicker than the novice.

The brain needs repetition and patterns so as to be able to send the necessary signals to the body. The key words here are 'rehearsal' and practice.

Tension can also affect co-ordination, particularly before a fight. Therefore the methods described here can be used as preparation for the fight itself.

Shadow-boxing

Shadow-boxing is fighting an imaginary opponent. All the skills of the ring are performed solo. This serves a number of functions, but particularly it acts as an aid to co-ordination, by allowing you to perform the skills over and over again without the pressure of fighting someone or the need to transmit speed and power to a target such as a focus pad or bag.

Problems such as balance and lack of fluidity can be gradually eroded. Individual or combination skills can be worked at a slow, medium or fast pace.

A by-product of shadow-boxing is mental rehearsal and it is this area that acts to overcome prefight tension.

You should imagine your opponent throwing particular techniques at you as you perform the necessary counter skills. Also you should 'see' the gaps in his defence and launch your own attacks. Eye, hand and foot should all combine to produce the skill required.

Guidelines for Co-ordination:

1) Perform all actions slowly at first. Build speed gradually.
2) Shadow-box for both rehearsal and repetition.
3) Erode the problems piece by piece so that your brain has a chance of learning what you expect of it.

Conditioning Summary

The aim of this chapter has been to make you 'fit to fight' and to that end it has been necessary to included much information on how and why. The silent question continually thrown up by the advice offered is 'when?'

What is required now is structure. The right frequency, the right duration, the right balance, and for that we need a schedule.

Chapter Nine: The Schedule

(Including nutrition/rest/weight control)

A kick boxer needs a structured plan for his training week and also for his training year. Into this plan must go his skills sessions, his running sessions, his strength sessions, his diet and allocated periods of rest.

The plan or schedule must be realistic, it must be achievable and above all it must produce the necessary results.

Notes and remarks should be made on each training session, these may be as brief or involved as you require.

The Basic Schedule

Schedules should be based around the idea of alternate-day training to prevent staleness and to allow recovery.

Monday	Run	Conditioning	Annotate Diary
Tuesday	Skills		" "
Wednesday	Run	Conditioning	" "
Thursday	Skills		" "
Friday	Run	Conditioning	" "
Saturday	Skills		" "
Sunday	Rest		

We have already given some indication of the frequency and duration of running in Chapter Eight, however, here we will break this down as a part of an overall training schedule together with suggested skills sessions.

These schedules show four levels of progression.

The reader may already be beyond some of the initial levels and may wish to enter the schedules where best appropriate.

Schedule One: [0 to 2 months]

Monday/Wednesday/Friday

2 mile steady state jog/run					
Press-ups	Dips	Curls	Sit-ups	Leg Raises	Crunches

2 miles x 3 per week for 8 weeks = 48 miles L.S.D.

Tuesday/Thursday/Saturday 1½ hours

Warm-up and Stretch	15 mins	
Focus Pads	25 mins	Primary punches
Shield	25 mins	Primary five body kicks
Pairs	25 mins	Basic defensive skills
Sunday	Rest	

Schedule Two: [2 to 6 months]

Monday/Wednesday/Friday

3 miles for first 6 weeks			4 miles for second 6 weeks		
5 miles for last 4 weeks					
Press-ups	Dips	Curls	Sit-ups	Leg Raises	Crunches

3 miles x 3 per week for 6 weeks	= 54 miles L.S.D.
4 miles x 3 per week for 6 weeks	= 72 miles L.S.D.
5 miles x 3 per week for 4 weeks	= 60 miles L.S.D.
plus 48 miles from schedule one	= 234 miles L.S.D. = Base + 34

Tuesday/Thursday/Saturday 1½ hours (approx)

Warm-up and Stretch	15 mins	
Shadow-boxing	3 x 2 mins	
Focus Pads	20 mins	Primary punches
Focus Pads	2 x 2 mins	Hands
Shield	20 mins	Primary five body kicks
Shield	2 x 2 mins	Kicks
Pairs	10 mins	Basic defensive skills
Sparring	2 x 2 mins	Hands
Sparring	2 x 2 mins	Hands and legs

Schedule Three: [6 months to 1 year]

Monday/Wednesday/Friday

Monday	5 miles L.S.D		Enter time in diary
Wednesday	2½ miles Fartlek		
Friday	3 miles medium/fast run		Enter time in diary
Press-ups	Dips	Curls	Sit-ups	Leg Raises	Crunches

Tuesday/Thursday/Saturday

Warm-up and Stretch	15 mins	
Shadow-boxing	3 x 2 mins	
Sparring	3 x 2 mins	Hands only
Sparring	3 x 2 mins	Hands and legs
Sparring	2 x 2 mins	Hands: on the wall
Sparring	2 x 2 mins	Hands and legs: tied
Focus Pads	2 x 2 mins	Hands primary/secondary
Shield	2 x 2 mins	Primary/secondary kicks
Focus Pad/Shield	20 mins	Additional skills

Schedule Four: [1 year plus]

Monday/Wednesday/Friday

Monday	5 miles L.S.D.	Enter time in diary
Wednesday	2½ miles Fartlek	
Friday	Interval session	

Tuesday/Thursday/Saturday

Warm-up and Stretch	15 mins	
Shadow-boxing	3 x 2 mins	
Sparring	4 x 2 mins	Hands only
Sparring	4 x 2 mins	Hands and legs
Sparring	2 x 2 mins	Toe-to-toe hands/legs
Sparring	2 x 2 mins	On the wall: hands/legs
Focus Pads	2 x 2 mins	Hands
Shield	2 x 2 mins	Kicks
Focus Pads/Shield	20 mins	Strengths/weaknesses

Note: Rest is an essential part of every schedule. We nominated Sunday, in schedule one as the day of rest and followed this through with schedules two, three and four, but naturally you must pick the best suited day. Failure to rest will lead to staleness and injury.

It is outside of the scope of this book to recommend the perfect schedule for everyone, however, the above four schedules give you a clear reference as to where you should be pitching your own training. Although schedules one and two may look modest at first sight, you should not underestimate the accumulative effects of day in, day out training.

The proof of a schedule's effectiveness is your gradual improvement. Progression though is frequently two steps forward and one back. Leaps forward are balanced by periods when, despite your best efforts, improvements slow or cease. For this reason schedules should cover a minimum of two months and a maximum of twelve.

Special Schedules

It may, from time to time, prove necessary to adopt a special schedule with the aim of producing a particular result. The six weeks building up to a fight for instance may have to reflect the skills needed to face a certain opponent.

Into this schedule might go skills sessions to counter your own perceived weaknesses and tactics to either foil your opponent's strengths or to capitalise on his weaknesses. At times like these your training diary is an invaluable source of information. The answers may well lie in what has gone before.

It is strongly recommended that a kick boxer should not enter the ring with less than one year's training (though 18 months is better). Exceptions to this rule are simply that, exceptions.

Fighters who come from different systems such as boxing or karate should be wary of the assumption that their skills will easily translate to the kick boxing ring. Although their previous training is an advantage over the complete novice, against more skilled fighters their areas of ignorance will be exposed.

Once you have started to fight regularly you will find that rigid long-term scheduling may prove difficult as you constantly address the needs of each fight, but once again the question that needs to be answered is . . . 'what am I training for?' You should identify the task and then construct the schedule that will deliver the result. The need for a capable and trusted coach is essential for the successful attainment of this.

The last schedule to be considered is the week leading up to the fight. There is a danger that the anxious fighter may wish to 'test' his fitness by doing a particularly long or strenuous run in the last week or that he will want to spar an excessive number of rounds so that psychologically he is reassured that he can 'go the distance'. This 'testing' is often the result of a failure to schedule properly and can drain a fighter at just the time when he needs to throttle back.

Fight Week Schedule

Monday	Run	Fartlek	Conditioning
Tuesday	Skills		
Wednesday	Run	3 miles easy	Conditioning
Thursday	Skills		
Friday	Run	2 miles easy	Stretch and Rest
Saturday	Shadow Boxing	5 rounds	Stretch and Rest
Sunday	Fight Day	Extra hour in bed	

The purpose of shadow-boxing on the day before the fight is to keep the visualisation strong without taxing the body.

The significance of the fight week schedule becomes more apparent when you compare it with schedule four - the fight week schedule should apply to all fighters irrespective of how experienced they are. You cannot get any fitter in one week, but you can exhaust yourself. Be disciplined.

Weight Control and Nutrition

Weight control is one of the most misunderstood areas of kick boxing. All too often dehydration is used as a means to make the correct weight for a fight. This is due to poor knowledge of what determines weight and weight loss.

Food is the fuel that powers the machine. Failure to take fuel on board quite simply means running out of 'gas'. Because of the huge energy requirements of kick boxing, (as many as 4,000 calories a day) crash dieting is out. Training, rest and nutrition must work in balance.

Here we will look at the basics of nutrition and show how to lose weight using two safe methods, calorific reduction spread over a given period, and a fat-controlled diet coupled with a fat-burning programme.

A Balanced Diet

A balanced diet should contain 55 per cent carbohydrates, 15 per cent protein and 30 per cent fat. The additional 5 per cent is allowance for alcohol. Kick boxing is a contact sport and as such it is considered that eating a little more protein will help build and repair the body better, so cut the alcohol to the bare minimum and take on board extra protein.

The odd pint of beer will not harm you and may well do some psychological good. After a particularly hard work-out a beer will assist the 'feel good' factor.

There are some good general 'rules of thumb' when considering nutrition:

1) Eat chicken, turkey and fish particularly tuna, in preference to red meat.

2) Cut down on sugar and fat consumption. Modern convenience foods contain large amounts of 'hidden' sugar and fats.

3) Avoid cakes, pastries and confectionary. Fill up on fresh fruit and tinned fruit in natural juice, not syrup.

4) Complex carbohydrates, such as pasta, bread, beans and cereals yield energy over a period of time and are therefore good for you. Simple carbohydrates containing refined sugar, such as chocolate, will give a short energy boost followed by a drop in blood sugar levels so avoid them.

5) Eat plenty of fresh vegetables for vitamins and fibre.

The Body Equation

The body requires 15 calories per pound of body weight daily in order maintain itself, thus a ten-stone man (140 lbs) needs 15 calories x 140 lbs = 2100 calories per day or 14,700 per week.

One pound of fat has 3,500 calories, therefore, in order to lose the safe average of 2 lbs per week, the body must reduce its weekly calorific intake by 7,000 calories or 1,000 calories daily. 2,100 calories minus 1,000 = 1100 daily or 7,700 calories weekly.

So, a ten stone man wishing to reduce his weight to say 9 stone 6 lbs for a fight would need 4 weeks to arrive at his target weight.

Another part of the equation is the burning of calories due to exercise. You burn approximately 100 calories per mile of running - true, if you run a five-minute mile you will burn more calories than at a ten-minute mile pace, but not that much.

A mile at a five-minute mile pace will burn about 105 calories per mile and a mile at a ten-minute pace will burn about 95 calories. This is because duration plays as large a part as speed in the total calorific burn.

So our 10-stone fighter trying to make 9st 6 lbs and running 3 miles every other day could afford to eat 900 extra calories a week and still maintain his 2 lbs a week weight loss.

3 miles equals 300 calories x 3 times a week = 900.

But a kick boxer does not only run. His conditioning work-outs and highly aerobic sparring and focus pad/shield rounds will also need to be added to the equation.

For every five rounds of sparring or pad/shield work, you should eat another 150 calories (5 rounds = 15 mins or 1½ x 100). It should be noted that even in the one-minute rest between rounds, your body is still burning calories at a high rate.

So, in order to work out what you should be eating, you should add up the number of miles of running per week, add up the number of rounds of sparring/pad work and then work out your calorific needs. Your best aid to this is of course your schedule.

The Body's Adjustment

After you have been on a diet for about three weeks your body will adjust its needs and slow down the metabolism so as not to starve. In order to defeat this after each three weeks you should up your calorific intake for about four or five days to trick the body into speeding up again. Then resume the diet.

Dehydration

Weight loss greater than 2 to 2 ½ lbs per week is dangerous. Weight loss induced by sweating is the most dangerous of all. Dehydration robs you of strength and can cause rapid fatigue in the ring. Further, the body is composed mainly of liquid and reducing by sweating means the loss of liquid everywhere in the body, including that cushioning the brain.

Dehydration is considered to be a chief component in brain damage to boxers. Its use as an aid to weight reduction is nothing less than playing Russian roulette.

Fat Reduction

A drawback with a calorie reducing programme is that unless you are careful you will be cutting down on the carbohydrates that you need for energy and the protein that you need to build and repair muscle. It is really surplus fat that needs to be targeted.

Fat is not a bad thing in itself. It performs many vital functions such as keeping your skin and arteries supple, balancing your hormonal levels and as a store for energy.

The kick boxers body should comprise of:
8 to 10 per cent fat for men
12 to 18 per cent fat for women

If we aim to achieve the above figures, then we must cut down on surplus fat rather than lean muscle. The obvious way to attempt this is diet.

Remove all sweets, chocolate, cakes, puddings, pastries and cut dairy produce to the absolute minimum. Fill up on tuna, turkey, chicken, fresh vegetables and fruit. The beauty of this method over a calorie-controlled diet is that you can eat considerable quantities of the above because it is fat control that we are after. You will never go hungry on this type of diet.

The second stage of fat control is to 'burn-off' the surplus and to do that we need to look at heart rates.

Heart Rates

In the past it was believed that the harder your heart worked, (strenuous effort such as fast running) then the more calories that you burnt, therefore the more weight that you would lose. Whereas in general terms this could be said to be true, it must also be said that the body has a number of energy systems and these burn different 'fuels'.

As it is fat that you want to lose, the rate at which your heart works will determine whether you burn carbohydrates or fats as a fuel. Training at 50 to 60 per cent of your maximum heart rate burns fat.

Your maximum heart rate is 220 minus your age. Therefore a twenty year old's maximum is 200. 50 to 60 per cent of this is 100 to 120 beats per minute. This is fast walking pace.

Below is a table which indicates your fat burning level by age.

20 years: 220 - 20 = 200; 50/60 per cent = 100/120 beats per minute

25 years: 220 - 25 = 195; 50/60 per cent = 97.5/117 beats per minute

30 years: 220 - 30 = 190; 50/60 per cent = 95/114 beats per minute

35 years: 220 - 35 = 185. 50/60 per cent = 92.5/111 beats per minute

40 years: 220 - 40 = 180; 50/60 per cent = 90/108 beats per minute

To count the number of beats per minute, place your fingers on either your radial pulse or your carotid pulse for 15 seconds then multiply by four. A far easier way is to obtain a pulse meter that can be strapped to your wrist like a watch for a continuous check.

45 to 60 minutes of fast walking three times per week will burn fat off leaving you leaner and lighter without loss of strength.

The sophisticated schedule should incorporate both diet and fat burning, eradicating forever the tendency to crash diet two weeks before a fight.

Summary

Skills, conditioning, diet and rest must work in balance and this is achieved by both keeping to a schedule and maintaining a training diary. Structure is necessary in order to cover all the bases. Haphazard training is pure indulgence and has no place in the routine of the would-be champion.

Progress takes time and commitment.

Weight control can be achieved without hunger or loss of strength providing it is planned over weeks and months. Aim for a 2 lb reduction per week.

Dehydration is dangerous because it robs you of strength and reduces the cushioning fluid around the brain thereby increasing the risk of brain damage.

In order for you to reach your maximum potential, you need a coach to teach, guide and support you. A good coach can pave the road to success.

Chapter Ten: The Coach

The role of the coach is to teach the fighter the skills of kick boxing, to guide his training by providing schedules and pre-fight planning, to debrief and analyse fight performance and to support, encourage and motivate the fighter to greater ability and success.

To be a coach is to take on responsibility for a fighter and to do everything possible to see that he or she reaches their potential. It is neither an ego trip nor a chance to re-live your own fight career.

In order to be successful, the coach must constantly update and deepen his knowledge in order to give his best to the fighters for whom he has responsibility.

Skill Development

All fighters are individuals and the coach must always balance the personal needs of a fighter with that of supplying a broad-based fight education.

Novices will of course require a sound grounding in the basic skills, but as the fighter progresses his own talents and weaknesses have to be addressed. Schedules are by their very nature individual and a constant source of reference for both coach and fighter.

A fighter's physical type, intelligence level, common sense, desire and consistency will affect how much he can be taught. This calls for a flexible approach.

In Chapters One, Two, Three and Four, we set out the primary and secondary, defensive and combination skills that must be taught first. Precisely how this is achieved is up to the individual coach, though it is fair to say the first six months of any kick boxer's training should be fairly standard.

What will not be standard is the ability of a fighter to absorb what is taught. It is when a fighter fails to make sufficient progress during group tuition that the coach must utilise specialised sessions to eradicate the problems. Patience, skill and ingenuity are called for when an otherwise promising fighter does not respond to a particular aspect of training.

Addressing individual needs is the most frustrating yet paradoxically the most rewarding of a coach's tasks. The formula for dealing with these needs is simple in theory, but frequently difficult in practice.

1) Identify the problem.
2) Make the fighter aware of it.
3) Use a combination of methods to cure it.
4) Monitor and record the improvement or its lack.
5) Use the situation to best advantage by building the trust between you.

An intelligent coach can turn a potentially negative situation into a positive one.

Fighter Selection

From day one of training a coach must be a 'talent spotter'. Many people wash up on the doors of a kick boxing gym, but only a few will be both sincere in their commitment and talented enough to be marked down as a potential fighter.

Surprises do occur however and there is a phenomenon known as the 'gym fighter'. This is an individual who performs very well in the gym, but is unable to reproduce the same skill in a contest.

Occasionally the reverse happens whereby a nondescript fighter grows in stature once 'between the ropes.' Generally speaking, the coach will have monitored a kick boxer for some months before making a decision about whether or not that person should fight. It must always be borne in mind that a fighter's safety is of paramount importance. Keenness is not a substitute for realism.

The schedules described in the previous chapter not only act as training regimes, but also as a means of uncovering potential fighters.

A coach should also keep his own coaching diary with entries for all the fighters in his gym. When coaching notes are matched against observation and video playback, most questions about ability will be answered.

Under the coach's guidance a fighter's natural style will develop, from which point on training becomes a case of accentuating the positive and eliminating the negative. Physical qualities will have a large bearing on this e.g. a long-legged and flexible man might be encouraged to develop kicking skills or a short powerful man taught to close rapidly using heavy punching combinations.

Whatever style in chosen, the coach must advise and listen. Good communication between the fighter and the coach is an absolute must. Both should feel happy that they know the aim and the purpose of each segment of training.

The Whole Fighter

The coach is responsible for developing the whole fighter - his mental as well as his physical skills. Up until now we have dealt only with the physical side of training - skill, speed, strength, stamina, flexibility and co-ordination.
The coach must make the fighter aware of mental skills and fashion training sessions that hone them.

Many of the mental skills can be paired with the physical in order to achieve a better understanding of their role.

Perception)
Anticipation)————— Speed
Reflex)

Perception is like an aura around the fighter whereby he 'senses' his opponent's intention and acts accordingly.

Anticipation is reading the 'signs' of an opponent – made much easier of course when the opponent 'telegraphs' his intent.

Reflex, as already described in Chapter Seven, is the mental speed that enables you to react correctly to a stimulus, i.e an opportunity or intention.

These three frequently work with each other and are best demonstrated by an experienced fighter bringing his skills to bear whilst under pressure.

Confidence)————— Strength

This is composure or fighting with integrity, whereby a fighter does not allow his opponent to throw him out of his stride. It is not bravado, but a demonstration of a fighter's belief in himself. It is often the best indicator of thorough preparation.

Determination)——— Stamina

The will to win has won many sporting battles. The striving for victory no matter how tough the opposition can wear down a superior opponent who is not prepared to go the extra mile.

Concentration)——— Accuracy

Keeping your concentration is very important, especially in the latter rounds of a fight when fatigue and pain blur your thinking. One lax moment can lead to disaster against a heavy hitter.

Mental Agility)————— Flexibility

This is the ability to make adjustments to your own fighting style when an opponent fights in an unorthodox or unexpected manner.

Visualisation)
Calculation)
Analysis)

Visualisation is a form of mental rehearsal and is widely practised in athletics. You imagine your opponent's skill, see your response and its success. The benefits of visualisation cannot be overestimated.

Calculation is the application of logic to the task in hand. A cold dispassionate appraisal of each situation.

Analysis is the weighing up of performance, both your own and an opponent's. Analysis is akin to calculation, the essential difference is that it is performed after the event rather than during.

Ruthlessness

This is not so much a mental skill as a character trait. If you cannot summon up enough ruthlessness in the ring then you have no business entering it in the first place.

★

The mental skills have many levels of appreciation and subtlety. They tend to be slower to develop than the physical skills, but this should not dissuade the coach from teaching them from the outset.

Their true value lies in turning a brawler into a tactician and a strategist. Someone who brings his greatest skills against an opponent's weakest edge. Someone who can reverse misfortune by staying objective in the teeth of adversity - a thinker!

The simplest and most effective way to get a fighter to think is to ask a question. By posing the problem the coach is asking the fighter to consider the options. Viable solutions are what you are after - there can be no right or wrong in the answer, only better alternatives. Skills, including mental skills, get sharper with use.

Debriefing sessions after training are particularly useful for getting the fighter to appreciate the mental aspects, e.g. select a particular problem that the fighter has just experienced whilst sparring and ask him to consider the options open to him. Steer him, don't lead him by the nose.

The Fighting Year

Having created a schedule for the fighter, the coach must now turn his attention to the broad year plan. In the case of a fighter just starting out, this will be simply a case of fighting followed by rest and assessment of performance before returning to the gym for further training.

Fighting every four to six weeks and allowing for a Christmas and midsummer break, will mean possibly as many as eight fights in the first year. (This is an upper limit. Four to five fights is perhaps nearer to the average.)

During this first year the coach will be learning much about the fighter as well as his own training methods. The goal is always to have a fighter progressing step by step with the risks kept to a minimum.

It is strongly recommended that a fighter is not asked to fight at a class higher than usual or for longer than normal until he has shown the ability to perform well and consistently. Build slowly and set the foundations deep.

After one year or eight fights, whichever comes later, the coach can start to construct a plan that will gradually carry the fighter towards regional, national and international championships. Not all fighters will aspire to or be capable of winning a championship, even a modest one such as a regional title. It cannot be stated strongly enough that a coach's greatest responsibility is the fighter's safety.

A potential champion however should have an agreed series of fights lined up so that each aspect of his skills is measured and his weaknesses eradicated under ring conditions.

The steady progress towards a championship is the most challenging and enjoyable time in a fighter/coach relationship.

Assessing the Fighter

A coach should know his fighter inside out - his character, his strengths and weaknesses, his stage of development, his lifestyle and the pressures within it that affect him as a fighter and last, but not least, his personal goals as a kick boxer.

Without this knowledge you might make the mistake of sending a man into the ring who is experiencing personal problems that prevent him from concentrating on the fight.

He should be able to trust you, use you as a sounding board. You are at all times a partnership and problems can make the bond between you stronger and the problems themselves more bearable for him because of this. By allowing himself to be taught by you he is displaying a trust that must be both respected and returned.

Club Ethos

Building a good club or team spirit is very much about creating a positive atmosphere in the gym. Club members should be confident that they are entering an environment where their skills will increase whilst their safety is guarded. It can never be a place of fear or intimidation.

Members should be encouraged to support each other and although friendly rivalry is a spur to improvement, the limits must be controlled by the coach.

Knowing that your team mates are at the ringside, cheering you on, can lift a fighter to new heights. The need to be part of a group and to have your place within it respected is necessary to all human beings, but especially those who face a potentially dangerous task.

Some coaches insist on all club members dressing the same, thereby showing both the club and the outside world that they are united, others choose less obvious methods and instead work at the somewhat harder task of making everybody realise that all ability is relative and each person has their own worth within the group and their own contribution to make.

My own coach was a master of understatement and saw himself as part of the group. The most important part for sure, but essentially just one of us. A good deal of his coaching was conducted by sparring with each fighter in turn. Instant feedback came by way of comments on your performance.

Whatever way is chosen, it is important that the coach build and maintain the club ethos. Its effect on the individual fighter cannot be overstated.

Assistant Coaches and Cornermen

Many coaches use assistants. These may be ex-fighters or simply long-term club members who wish to pass on what they have learnt. Frequently it is these people that assist in the corner during a fight.

The coach may choose to make such an assistant responsible for a particular area of training or to work with a fighter on a series of skills. This enables the coach to detach himself from the central teaching role and circulate around the gym observing and recording.

An assistant coach is sometimes a halfway step to becoming a coach in your own right - a form of apprenticeship. During this 'apprenticeship' you will have a golden opportunity to observe both sides of the teaching process. Much can be learnt in this phase and you should of course keep notes.

Ideas on how to improve and develop facets of training will occur and it may be that the coach will give his permission for you to try out some of these ideas within his gym. The role of assistant coach is a valuable one.

Cornermen or seconds help the coach to service the fighter between rounds. The tasks they perform are essential to the fighter and each part of the cornerman team must understand his job, which should be allocated by the coach before the fight. The fighter must know who the cornerman team are in advance and have confidence in them.

A slick professional team can perform all the functions necessary to prepare the fighter for the next round including:

1) Providing both the stool, water and bowl before the fighter reaches the corner at the end of the round.

2) Providing the towel to both remove surplus water and to 'fan' the fighter.

3) Providing the adrenalin to staunch bleeding and an 'iron' to smooth out swellings to the cheeks and eyes.

Only one person, the coach himself, should give advice between rounds. The advice must be simple, realistic and brief. Constructive in-fight analysis is an art in itself and the mark of a good coach. The urge to 're-train' the fighter between rounds should be resisted. Essentially a fighter's needs and order of priority are these:

1) Air
2) Water
3) Advice.

The language used in advice should be familiar to the fighter, simple reminders of that worked at in the gym and delivered in a calm clear voice without excessive emotion.

Post-Fight Debriefing

Irrespective of whether or not a fighter wins his contest, the coach should resist making comments on a fighter's performance other than simple congratulations or sympathy.

On stepping out of the ring the fighter full of adrenalin and perhaps emotional. He is not in a position to appreciate or learn from a coach's observations at this time.

The time and place for the debriefing is two days after the event, when a more objective view can be taken by all concerned.

The purpose of the debriefing is to improve a fighter. He should not be allowed to think that victory alone is the aim. In the case of defeat the positive should be emphasised and the fighter made to realise that much can be learnt from what appears to be a negative performance.

Lessons may have to be relearnt or re-emphasised before the next fight. Video recordings are invaluable in post-fight debriefing sessions.

The formula for debriefings is as follows:

1) Observe the fault.

2) Discuss the reasons for it and the possible solutions.

3) Construct training sessions that eradicate the problem.

★

Chapter Eleven:
The Way Beyond Trophies

Martial arts are complex, highly technical creations that originated on the battlefield. Throughout the centuries many systems evolved, both armed and unarmed and along the way it became recognised that the benefits bestowed by their practice went beyond merely physical protection.

It has long been acknowledged that their highest worth lies in acting as a vehicle by which a person tests both their mind and their body with the aim of producing a better human being.

Martial sports such as judo, karate-do and kick boxing are descended from the battlefield arts and the benchmark of their success lies in sporting victory. However, the training, testing and trials of kick boxing can be severe. The kick boxer must continually prove his worth, at risk of physical injury.

The commitment, hard and often lonely training, the harsh reality of defeat and the consequent long road back, can be a character-building process by which a person can shape their life outside the ring. To this extent kick boxing can be considered a martial art. To many people, kick boxing is controversial. This is not hard to appreciate. The sight of two people fighting, especially with skill is, and always has been, regarded as potentially dangerous to society and the permitting of it, albeit in a stylised form, suspect.

The fear of course is that the skills learnt in the gym will spill out into the streets, where the public would be at risk. Nothing could be further from the truth. The time it takes to learn such skill is the perfect deterrent to any thug, who can easily purchase a knife or hammer from any hardware store or perhaps even obtain a gun and be infinitely more of a threat to society.

Indeed the crime figures of all western democracies bear this out and ironically, in the east, where many of the martial arts evolved, street crime is at a much lower level and the use of martial arts to intimidate, hurt and rob people is practically unheard of.

The question remains however, why does man indulge in combat sports? Man is an evolved ape, who, for all his striving has yet to rid himself of the animal within. Our emotions are inextricably bound up with the need for territory, to procreate and to survive. And of all of these needs, it is survival that is the greatest. In this respect man, for all his intellect, has not progressed beyond his primitive ancestors, the hunter-gatherers.

This survival instinct manifests itself in many ways, but the one that causes the most disquiet is aggression. All to often man, the most aggressive species on the planet, lets his aggression get out of control and the proof of that is in any daily news bulletin.

We have to find channels for our animal instincts, but first we must be honest enough to admit their existence.

Kick boxing has the potential to be a force for good in the broader aspects of life, a hard challenging pursuit that allows the hunter-gatherer within us to express itself, but safely, within a rule structure and ultimately with the idea that there are bigger arenas than the ring.

For a number of years now there have been attempts to outlaw professional boxing on medical, ethical and humanitarian grounds. Kick boxing, having a smaller public profile, has as yet escaped the attention of the opposition movements. This may change in the future.

The medical arguments against are irrefutable. Blows to the head do cause brain damage, but then again so does falling from a mountain, crashing a racing car, an unopened parachute and so on.

The ethical arguments centre around whether or not doctors, as people who give their lives to saving the injured should be participating in boxing and kick boxing by giving pre-fight medicals and post-fight care.

Against this we might argue that smokers should also be refused medical help or for that matter anyone who wilfully engages in a dangerous sport, drinks too much or lets themselves become overweight through overeating.

The humanitarian grounds are basic. It is reasoned that human beings should not deliberately cause each other injury whatever the excuse, and in any case certainly not for public entertainment. The argument against this is just as basic, you cannot legislate away man's very nature. It amounts to sitting on a throne and commanding the waves to go back.

Failure to acknowledge what we are is wilful blindness. It is not the skill of kick boxers that represents a danger, but rather the motivations of individuals.

If we were to outlaw activities on the basis of their potential harm then clearly we must start with politics, which has seen millions die this century alone, for the aggrandisement of dictators and their regimes.

There is however a clear and pressing case for the control of kick boxing. Abuse of its skills is indefensible. There is a duty on all coaches and instructors to instil discipline and a sense of responsibility on anyone taking up the sport. Those unable to display the necessary maturity should be denied training.

There is a Latin maxim which has become synonymous with sport, 'A healthy mind in a healthy body' yet the original Greek does not read the same as the Roman translation and is perhaps more apt for the kick boxer, 'Civilize the mind, make savage the body.'

I believe it is an aim to which we should all aspire.

Appendix

Targets and Techniques

The target areas in kick boxing are the front and sides of the head and trunk down to the waistline of the leggings. (Diagrams 54 and 55)

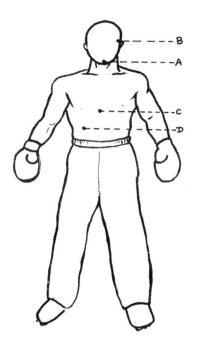

Diagram 54

Diagram 55

Striking outside of this area is a foul and will meet with first a warning, then a point deduction and finally disqualification.

Because there are spinning techniques in kick boxing it is entirely possible to accidently hit an illegal area, however, the referee's decision in cases of dispute is always final. Protest can attract additional penalty points or in extreme cases, disqualification.

Sweeping techniques may be performed at boot height only.

Techniques are considered legal when they strike with the glove, boot or shin. Using the forearm, elbow, knee or head are fouls.

The main targets for a knockout are:

1) The chin (A) – struck either from the side or from underneath.

2) The temple (B) – struck from the side.

3) The solar plexus (C) – struck straight in or rising upwards.

4) The liver (D) – struck straight in or rising upwards.

for more kick boxing
and martial arts books, visit

www.summersdale.com